🐓 100 🐓 Favorite Chicken Dishes

100 Favorite Chicken Dishes

PATRICIA TENNISON

CONTEMPORARY
BOOKS

CHICAGO

Library of Congress Cataloging-in-Publication Data

Tennison, Patricia.
  100 favorite chicken dishes / Patricia Tennison.
      p.   cm.
    ISBN 0-8092-4479-9 (pbk.) :
    1. Cookery (Chicken)   I. Title.   II. Title: One hundred favorite
chicken dishes.
  TX750.5.C45T46   1991
  641.6'65—dc20   91-6560
                                                                      CIP

Published by Contemporary Books, Inc.
180 North Michigan Avenue, Chicago, Illinois 60601
Manufactured in the United States of America
International Standard Book Number: 0-8092-4479-9

To my ever-supportive family, Tom, Jeff, and Ashley

CONTENTS

PART II • THE RECIPES

ACKNOWLEDGMENTS

Heartfelt thanks to colleague JeanMarie Brownson for her generous help in the kitchen and for her impressive foodstyling on the cover. Bill Hogan, again, is our ever-smiling man behind the camera, and his work illustrates his talent with food.

A special thanks to editor Nancy Crossman at Contemporary Books, who wisely guided the book's direction, and to Emily Pearl and Leah Mayes for carefully fine-tuning the copy. Georgene Sainati leaves her stylish imprint with a little chick here and little chick there.

And most important, loving thanks to my husband, Tom, and children, Jeff and Ashley, for the 100 ways they show support.

INTRODUCTION

Americans eat almost twice the amount of chicken per person that they ate twenty-five years ago. And with good reason.

Chicken is a perennial favorite, a culinary chameleon as homespun as chicken noodle soup or as elegant as chicken breasts with macadamia nuts. Mild-tasting chicken appeals to people of all ages, who appreciate it straight and plain or dressed with zesty herbs and spices.

Because the supply is plentiful, chicken is a low-cost source of protein compared to beef. Compared to other meats, chicken is also particularly healthful—low in sodium, calories, and saturated fats.

Chicken's latest appeal, however, may be convenience. In addition to whole fryers, shoppers can now choose a variety of cut-up and boneless forms. Chicken breasts come whole, split, with bones, boneless, and with or without skin. Chicken legs are available whole or split. You can even find a couple of pounds of chicken wings packaged and ready to cook.

Chicken also responds well to a variety of cooking methods. This book gives you many options: baking, broiling, simmering, stir-frying, and microwaving. Microwaving is especially useful for today's fast lifestyles, so about half of the conventional recipes in this book include microwave instructions as well. For some recipes, such as fast and flavorful One-Plate Chicken and Vegetables, where everything cooks at the same time on one plate, the unique microwave technique stands alone.

I've arranged the recipes into chapters that I hope will be helpful. Need something really fast? Zoom to "Quick Picks," where most of the dishes, such as Country-Mustard Drumsticks, can be on the table in 10 minutes flat. The "Light Fare" recipes, which use lots of tricks to avoid extra fats, also tend to be quite fast.

When you have extra time, perhaps on the weekends, thumb through the "Casseroles" and "Real Meals" chapters. Most of these dishes, such as Almond Chicken and Rice or Whole Turkey with Apple-Walnut Dressing, are ideal for "planned leftovers," which in the long run save you lots of time.

The recipes in "Company's Coming" are not necessarily more time-consuming or complex than others in the book. But they do offer more unusual or expensive ingredients such as duck, pine nuts, blue cheese, or passion fruit. Adult tastes, you might say.

"Kid Stuff" leans the other way. Easy-to-like ingredients such as carrots, apples, and corn make these simple dishes especially appealing to children.

When you eat a lot of chicken like we do in my family, you have leftovers. You'll find plenty of ideas for those leftovers in the "Salads" chapter. "Soups" offers recipes from scratch or from the can. The "Appetizers" recipes draw on spices and peppers to get appetites rolling.

"Micro-Grilling" is an exciting chapter. Charcoal-grilled chicken can be ready in a fraction of the time (and will be juicier, too) if you cook the chicken first in the microwave oven, then put it on the grill briefly for that wonderful grilled flavor. Turkey and duck are delicious prepared this way, too.

PART I
THE BASICS

CHICKEN

> **CHICKEN BUYING GUIDE**
>
> *Fryer-broiler:* Young tender bird that weighs 1½ to 3½ pounds ready to cook. This is the most common chicken found in supermarkets. May be roasted, baked, fried, grilled, or broiled.
>
> *Roaster:* Tender bird that weighs 3½ to 5 pounds ready to cook. May be roasted or baked.
>
> *Stewing chicken:* Older, less tender bird weighing 2½ to 5 pounds ready to cook. It has more fat than a fryer or roaster and is particularly good for soups. Usually stewed or otherwise cooked in liquids.
>
> *Capon:* Castrated male chicken weighing 5 to 7 pounds ready to cook. It has plenty of flavorful, tender meat. Usually roasted.
>
> *Cornish game hen:* Smallest member of the chicken family, weighing 1½ pounds or less ready to cook. May be roasted, baked, fried, grilled, or broiled.

PREPARING CHICKEN SAFELY

Some commonsense precautions are necessary when working with fresh products such as chicken. They are the same precautions that mothers have carefully taught for generations, and they prove how wise good cooking habits can be.

Chicken should always be cooked thoroughly before it is eaten. This doesn't mean you have to overcook it until it is dry and tough. But you do want the chicken fully cooked. The internal temperature should be 180°F; that is, the meat should all have turned from a pinkish to whitish color, and the juices should run clear, not pink.

The reason for the precaution is that raw chicken may contain salmonella bacteria, which thrives in warm, protein-rich environments. Thorough cooking kills the salmonella bacteria.

To start, wash your hands with warm water and soap before and after handling raw chicken. Keep your working area clean, and be sure not to put other foods or cooked chicken on the same spot where you just had the raw chicken. For example, when grilling, don't put the cooked chicken on the same plate that carried the raw chicken without washing the plate first. Use paper towels to clean the counters and work area.

When cutting raw chicken, use a nonporous plastic board, not a wooden board. Wooden boards are difficult to clean thoroughly. Wash all utensils and your cutting board thoroughly with a mild bleach-and-water solution.

Thaw chicken overnight in the refrigerator, or in cold water, or on the defrost cycle in the microwave oven. Do not let the chicken stand on the kitchen counter to defrost. Refrigerate or cook the thawed chicken right away.

STORING CHICKEN

Fresh chicken should be wrapped in plastic wrap or a plastic bag to prevent the juices from dripping and stored in the coldest (usually the back) part of the refrigerator. Do not chop chicken until it is ready to use. Wash well with cold water before cooking.

Cook fresh chicken within two to three days. Cooked chicken may be kept covered in the refrigerator for up to three days.

DEFROSTING CHICKEN

The microwave oven is a wonderful device for defrosting chicken. Place the frozen chicken in the microwave oven in its plastic bag or freezer paper. Use the *defrost* setting if your machine has one. If not, use the lowest setting and alternate two minutes cooking time with two minutes standing time. Remove the paper or plastic wrappings and tray as soon as they loosen. Turn and separate the chicken for even defrosting, taking care that it does not begin to cook. If parts such as the legs of a whole bird appear to start cooking, shield them loosely with smooth strips of aluminum foil to deflect the microwaves.

Pour off any juices that accumulate as you defrost. For large birds, place frozen meat on a rack so that the bird doesn't sit in the juices.

If you have time, defrost the chicken until it is just pliable, then place it in the refrigerator to finish defrosting.

The amount of defrosting time will vary depending on the size and shape of the meat, but roughly calculate 6 to 7 minutes per pound. Breasts and thighs take longer to defrost than drumsticks and wings. A pound of boneless chicken breasts, for example, takes about 12 minutes to defrost to just pliable. Another half hour in the refrigerator and they are ready to cook.

A few ice crystals will remain on just-defrosted chicken. These will disappear when you rinse the chicken and let it stand for a few minutes.

When the chicken is completely defrosted, cook it right away or refrigerate.

Do not freeze uncooked stuffed chicken or turkey. Do not refreeze thawed chicken.

BONING AND SKINNING CHICKEN

To reduce fat dramatically, skin chicken before eating. The skin from chicken breasts and thighs comes off quite easily—just grab it with your fingers and yank it off. For that final tug on often-stubborn drumsticks, use a paper towel for a better grip. Chicken wings are too much trouble to skin and usually are just left alone.

To bone chicken breasts, start at the tip portion where the meat is the thinnest. Use a small knife to cut away the bone as you gently pull the meat with your other hand.

ARRANGING CHICKEN IN THE MICROWAVE OVEN
Chicken should be arranged with the thickest portions to the outside of the casserole, plate, or dish for more even cooking. The bony ends of drumsticks, for example, should point toward the center.

Chicken thighs and drumsticks take longer to cook than breasts and wings. When cooking a whole, cut-up chicken, you may want to give the thighs and drumsticks a 1- to 2-minute head start in the microwave oven. Then arrange the chicken in a casserole so that the slowest-cooking pieces receive the most microwaves: thighs and drumsticks in the corners, breasts along the sides, and wings in the center.

COVERING CHICKEN IN THE MICROWAVE OVEN
Chicken pieces usually cook more evenly in the microwave oven if they are covered. Plastic wrap, vented, provides fast, moist cooking; waxed paper allows more moisture to escape and often prevents chicken from giving off as much juice. Different recipes will call for different coverings.

I prefer cooking whole chicken uncovered. I find that this gives a more roasted, rather than stewed, texture to the chicken. Also, small boneless strips of chicken may be cooked uncovered for a more stir-fried texture.

MICROWAVE POWER LEVELS
I find that most chicken dishes—even a whole broiler—cook best in the microwave oven on high power. The fast cooking speed retains juices best, and you get the bonus of the fastest possible cooking time.

When cooking larger birds, such as turkeys, reduce the power to medium. This allows the thicker portions to cook before the outer portions are overcooked.

HOW LONG TO COOK CHICKEN
Cooking time varies according to the weight, shape, and thickness of the chicken. As a rule, chicken takes about 6 to 8 minutes per pound in a 600- to 700-watt microwave oven. However, thick pieces and whole chicken take slightly longer; thin or cut-up pieces take less time. Boneless chicken breasts need only 5 minutes in the broiler. A cut-up whole chicken needs a good 45 minutes in a conventional oven.

HOW TO TELL WHEN CHICKEN IS DONE
How do I know when chicken is done? This has to be the most frequently asked question about chicken cooked by any method.

A perfectly cooked piece of chicken will have turned from pink to white in color and the juices will run clear, but the meat will still be moist. The internal temperature should be 180°F.

Test for doneness just before the recipe's lowest suggested cooking time. Use a knife to probe the chicken gently in its thickest portion, preferably near a bone, if any. Or prick the meat with a fork to make the juices run. When the meat has turned from pink to white and the juices run clear, the chicken is done.

COOKING CHICKEN BREASTS

Boneless chicken breasts are easy to prepare, easy to portion, and easy to cook—and thus very popular with busy cooks.

A whole chicken breast is made up of two halves that typically are split to make two servings. For the recipes in this book, then, one whole chicken breast equals two halves; two whole chicken breasts equals four halves.

In the microwave oven, place breasts skin side down. Arrange the thicker parts of the breasts to the outside of the plate. Cook the breasts covered with plastic wrap, vented, on high power. With high power, the chicken loses very little juice (about half as much as when cooked on medium power), resulting in a moist, tender meat.

Thicker breasts will take a little longer per pound to cook than thinner ones.

COOKING CHICKEN LEGS

In the microwave oven, arrange the legs so that the meatier portions face the outside and the thinner, bony ends point inward. Rearrange them midway through cooking, if necessary. Cook chicken legs tightly covered with plastic wrap, vented, on high power. With high power, the chicken legs retain more natural juices than when cooked at lower power.

COOKING WHOLE BIRDS

Whole chickens cook up beautifully both in the conventional oven and in the microwave oven. In the microwave oven, the meat is very moist, and because the chicken is in the microwave for about 20 minutes, the skin turns a light yellow color. (You can add more color and crispness by then putting the chicken in a very hot—400°F—conventional oven for a few minutes.)

Place the whole chicken, breast side down, in a 13" × 9" casserole. Do not cover. MICROWAVE (high) 17 to 22 minutes, until the meat is no longer pink and the juices run clear; turn over to breast side up after 10 minutes. Let stand until temperature registers 180°F.

Capons, whole ducks, and even small (10- to 12-pound) turkeys also do beautifully both in the conventional oven and in the microwave oven. For more even cooking in the microwave oven, you will want to cook larger birds such as turkeys on medium power. See the index for recipes.

Stuffing will not change the cooking time for the birds. For health-safety reasons, do not stuff birds until you are ready to cook them.

COMBINATION COOKING

Match your microwave oven with other cooking equipment to overcome some of the microwave oven's failings.

For better color on roast chicken or duck, put the microwave-cooked bird in a very hot conventional oven for 10 minutes to brown and crisp the skin. For quick-grilled chicken, cook first in the microwave oven then finish on a grill for that unique charcoal flavor.

TIPS FOR COOKING CHICKEN

- Before cooking, briefly pound a chicken or turkey breast half to help even its shape. This will help the piece cook more evenly.
- To remove skin from chicken parts, dry the pieces first with paper towels. Use your hands to pull off the skin. Use paper towels to grasp the skin and make the final pull from a chicken leg.
- For safety reasons, stuffing should be cooked first.
- Start slower-cooking parts such as thighs and legs first, then add breasts and wings.
- Chicken is done when the internal temperature reaches 180°F or the juices run clear rather than pink.
- Out of lemon? Substitute fresh lime juice or orange juice.
- Use leftover chicken to make a first-class sandwich or as the focal point of a salad.
- Save uncooked bones, wing tips, and necks in a plastic bag in the freezer until you have enough to make homemade chicken stock.
- Serve white chicken breasts on dark plates for better presentation.

SPECIAL MICROWAVING TIPS

- When you pull back the plastic wrap from a plate of chicken pieces to create vents, pick spots at opposite ends between the chicken pieces so that the chicken is still covered. This keeps the chicken moist, while allowing air pressure to escape.
- Make two vents—not just one. I find that this keeps juices from boiling hard, so that the chicken remains tender.
- Defrost chicken or turkey completely before cooking.
- Use high power for chicken pieces, whole fryers, and duck. It's not only fast, but the quick cooking also holds in juices.
- Use a combination of high power, then medium power, for larger birds such as capons and turkeys. This promotes more even cooking.
- Cook chicken livers on medium power. This keeps them from exploding.
- Remember to allow for standing time. Chicken will continue to cook for several minutes after you remove it from the microwave oven. Take this time into account when you judge for doneness.
- Salt chicken *after* cooking. Salt attracts microwaves and can cause uneven cooking if applied directly on chicken before cooking. This won't be as much of a problem if the salt is dissolved in enough cooking liquid or a sauce.
- A larger mass of food takes longer to cook in the microwave oven. If you double a recipe, add one-half more time and check for doneness.
- Thicker shapes take longer to cook than thin ones. Position thicker parts toward the outside of the dish where they will receive more microwave energy.

- Start whole chickens breast side down and turn them over 'midway for more even cooking.
- For chicken parts, start with thicker portions to the outside. Turn over and rearrange midway through cooking for more even results.
- Start slower-cooking parts such as thighs and legs first, then add breasts and wings.
- For soups and sauces, stir cooked, outside portions to the inside.
- Use small pieces of aluminum foil to shield areas that you don't want to cook or overcook, such as the wing tips of a whole capon or turkey. This is also a good technique if you want to defrost only a few slices of bacon.
- Stuffing will not appreciably affect cooking time.
- For crisp skin, cook the chicken, turkey, or parts completely in the microwave oven, then put under a conventional broiler or on a grill for a few minutes.
- When you are cooking chicken and vegetables together, arrange larger, slower-cooking vegetables, such as carrots and broccoli florets, on the outside of the dish for more even cooking. Faster-cooking vegetables, such as thin asparagus, mushrooms, bell peppers, scallions, or zucchini sticks, may be placed in the center.
- Microwave vegetables until slightly limp and easy to pierce before putting on a skewer with chicken for kabobs.
- If an accompanying sauce takes more than a few minutes to make, prepare the sauce before you cook the chicken and keep it warm.
- Reheat chicken on medium or medium-low power.
- Many wooden spoons may be left right in the bowl when cooking in a microwave oven and remain cool to the touch. However, I find that old wooden spoons that have darkened from age and oil do get quite hot. Experiment carefully.
- To remove odors from your microwave oven, place a cut lemon in a custard cup and MICROWAVE (high) 1 minute.

NUTRITIONAL BREAKDOWN BY PARTS
(Roasted Chicken, No Skin)

	½ Breast (86 grams)	1 Thigh (52 grams)	1 Drumstick (44 grams)	1 Wing (22 grams)
Protein	26.7 g	13.5 g	12.5 g	6.4 g
Calories	142	109	76	43
Total fat	3.07 g	5.7 g	2.5 g	1.7 g
Cholesterol	73 mg	49 mg	41 mg	18 mg
Sodium	63 mg	46 mg	42 mg	19 mg
Iron	.9 mg	.7 mg	.6 mg	.2 mg

Data source: U.S. Department of Agriculture

MICROWAVE CHICKEN COOKING CHART

Type	Amount	Covering	Power	Cooking Time, in Minutes	Special Instructions
Whole Chicken					
Whole (2½ pounds)	1	none	high	17–22	Place breast side down in 13″ × 9″ casserole; turn over after 10 minutes.
Split (2½ pounds)	1	plastic, vented	high	12–15	Place skin side down, drumsticks to outside in 13″ × 9″ casserole; turn over after 8 minutes.
Cut-up (2½ pounds)	1	plastic, vented	high	11–16	Cook thighs 1–2 minutes. In 13″ × 9″ casserole, put thighs and legs in corners, breasts on sides, wings in middle. Turn pieces over midway.
Chicken Parts					
Breasts, bone in	1	plastic, vented	high	2–3	
	2	plastic, vented	high	3–5	Arrange thickest portion to outside; rotate and turn after 2 minutes.
	4	plastic, vented	high	7–9	Arrange thickest portion to outside; rotate and turn after 5 minutes.
Breasts, boneless	1	plastic, vented	high	2–3	
	2	plastic, vented	high	3–4	Arrange thickest portion to outside; rotate and turn after 1½ minutes.
	4	plastic, vented	high	4–6	Arrange thickest portion to outside; rotate and turn after 2 minutes.
Legs, whole	1	plastic, vented	high	4–7	
	2	plastic, vented	high	5–8	Arrange thickest portion to outside; rotate and turn after 3 minutes.
	4	plastic, vented	high	8–10	Arrange thickest portion to outside; rotate and turn after 5 minutes.

Thighs, bone in	1	plastic, vented	high	3–4	
	2	plastic, vented	high	4–6	Rotate and turn after 2 minutes.
	4	plastic, vented	high	7–9	Rotate and turn after 4 minutes.
Thighs, boneless	1	plastic, vented	high	1–2	
	2	plastic, vented	high	2–3	Rotate and turn after 1 minute.
	4	plastic, vented	high	3–4	Rotate and turn after 1½ minutes.
	8	plastic, vented	high	4–6	Rotate and turn after 2 minutes.
Drumsticks	1	plastic, vented	high	2–3	
	2	plastic, vented	high	3–5	Turn over after 1½ minutes.
	4	plastic, vented	high	5–7	Arrange in spokelike fashion, thick ends to outside. Turn over after 3 minutes.
	8	plastic, vented	high	8–10	Arrange in spokelike fashion, thick ends to outside. Turn over after 4 minutes.
Wings	2	plastic, vented	high	2–3	
	4	plastic, vented	high	3–4	Arrange in a circle.
	8	plastic, vented	high	4–5	Arrange in a circle.
	12	plastic, vented	high	10–12	Arrange in a single layer in 13" × 9" casserole.

PART II
THE RECIPES

APPETIZERS

Appetizers, if they are true to their name, should be tempting morsels that whet but do not overwhelm the appetite, samplings small in size but generous in taste.

That, of course, is the diner's point of view. From the cook's point of view, it also helps if the appetizers are easy to make, so that attention can be drawn instead to the guests or at least to the next course.

Bearing in mind these two points of view—taste and ease of preparation—I've selected chicken appetizers that are especially appropriate for today's cook. Some of these appetizers can be made ahead. Others make frugal use of equipment to avoid heavy cleanup.

The chameleonlike personality of chicken makes it suitable for a variety of appetizers, from zesty Chicken Salsa to rich Chicken Liver Pâté.

For other appetizer ideas, browse through the "Soups" and "Salads" chapters for dishes such as Chicken-Spinach Soup, Tortilla-Lime Soup, Chicken-Asparagus Salad, and Macadamia-Chicken Salad.

CHICKEN SATAY WITH PEANUT DIP

Satay is basically Indonesian barbecue: bits of meat, fish, chicken, or vegetables served with a dipping sauce. Here, chicken strips are skewered and served with a peanut sauce—a typical dipping sauce found in Thai restaurants.

The chicken can be marinated and the sauce made twenty-four hours ahead and kept in the refrigerator. Reheat the sauce to room temperature before serving.

Preparation time: 15 minutes
Marinating time: 30 minutes
Cooking time: 6 minutes
Serves: 4–6

2 tablespoons shallots, minced
1 tablespoon vegetable oil
1 small red or green hot pepper, minced
¼ teaspoon ground turmeric
¼ teaspoon ground or whole cumin seeds
¼ teaspoon salt
½ cup unsweetened coconut milk
2 whole chicken breasts (4 halves), skinned, boned, and cubed
½ cup chunky peanut butter
1 teaspoon cider vinegar

1. Mix shallots, oil, hot pepper, turmeric, cumin, and salt in a small, nonstick skillet. Cook and stir over low heat about 2 minutes, until shallots soften. Stir in half (¼ cup) of the coconut milk.
2. Put chicken in a medium bowl. Stir in 3 tablespoons of the spices-and-coconut-milk mixture. Cover and let marinate in the refrigerator 30 minutes to 24 hours.
3. Mix remaining ¼ cup coconut milk, peanut butter, and vinegar into spice mixture. Heat over medium-low heat until bubbling; mixture will appear curdled, but this is authentic. The dip should be very thick and served warm.
4. Skewer chicken on bamboo skewers or toothpicks so that pieces are not touching. Broil on oiled broiler pan about 6 minutes, until centers of chicken pieces are no longer pink, turning once. Serve with dip on the side.

TIP: This recipe tastes special and exotic because of a number of special ingredients:
    Shallots. *Tastewise, a cross between onion and garlic, but more expensive than either. They're lovely, but you can substitute 2 tablespoons minced onion and 1 teaspoon minced garlic.*

Turmeric. *A beautifully colored ground herb that imparts an orange-yellow color and what I call a base flavor (a quiet, deep tone—not sharp if used in small amounts). If you leave it out, you'll miss a little color and a little taste. It keeps well on the spice rack. And a half teaspoon mixed into the water when making rice turns plain rice into a golden dish. Worth looking into.*

Cumin. *This little brown seed helps define Indonesian cooking and is a basic ingredient in curries as well as Mexican chilies and European cheese and sauerkraut dishes. It comes ground or in seeds, which hold their flavor longer. Without it, the peanut butter tastes like, well, peanut butter. Worth buying.*

Coconut Milk. *If you can only find the sweetened version, use ¼ cup coconut milk and ¼ cup milk.*

TIP: *Soak bamboo skewers in water to cover for 20 minutes before using. This prevents them from burning.*

CHICKEN NACHOS

Mixed with fresh zucchini and tomatoes, these chicken nachos are a wonderfully messy dish to eat with your fingers.

Preparation time: 20 minutes
Cooking time: 25 minutes
Serves: 4–6

2 **whole chicken breasts (4 halves), skinned and boned**
1 **cup water**
1 **tablespoon fresh lemon juice**
¼ **cup chopped onion**
1 **teaspoon minced garlic**
1 **tablespoon olive oil**
1 **pound zucchini, cut into ⅜-inch slices**
2–3 **ripe tomatoes, skinned, seeded, and chopped, or 1 16-ounce can tomatoes, drained and chopped**
1 **teaspoon minced fresh hot pepper or 6 good shakes hot pepper sauce**
¼ **teaspoon ground cumin**
¼ **teaspoon dried oregano**
½ **teaspoon salt**
⅛ **teaspoon freshly ground black pepper**
Tortilla chips
1 **cup grated cheddar**
¼ **cup chopped fresh coriander (cilantro)**
Sliced pickled jalapeño peppers

1. Put chicken, water, and lemon juice into a large, nonstick skillet. Heat to simmer; cover and simmer about 6 minutes, until chicken is no longer pink and juices run clear. Strain (reserve broth for other use, if desired); cool.
2. Put onion, garlic, and olive oil in same nonstick skillet. Cook and stir about 3 minutes, until onion is soft. Stir in zucchini, tomatoes, hot pepper, cumin, oregano, salt, and pepper. Cover. Cook and stir about 12 minutes, until zucchini is crisp-tender.
3. Dice chicken. Add to zucchini mixture. Cook and stir until heated through, about 3 minutes. Spread over tortilla chips. While still warm, sprinkle with cheese, cilantro, and jalapeño pepper slices.

MICROWAVE OVEN METHOD—12 minutes: (1) Put chicken in a 2-quart rectangular casserole. Eliminate the 1 cup water. Sprinkle with lemon juice. Cover with waxed paper. MICROWAVE (high) 5–7 minutes, until center is no longer pink, turning over once. Drain. Set aside. (2) Put onion, garlic, and olive oil in same 2-quart casserole. MICROWAVE (high) 1–2 minutes. Stir in zucchini, tomatoes, hot pepper, cumin, oregano, salt, and pepper. Cover. MICROWAVE (high) 4–6 minutes, until zucchini is just tender, stirring twice. Dice chicken. Add to zucchini mixture. Do not cover. MICROWAVE (high) 2–3 minutes to heat through. Finish as in Step 3 above.

TIP: *This recipe can be made with 1½ cups leftover cooked or grilled chicken.*

TIP: *Leftover mixture can be put into a toasted flour tortilla for a quick burrito.*

CHICKEN SALSA

Firm, tart tomatillos are the base of this terrific-tasting green salsa with chicken. Serve it with tortilla chips for a light, healthful appetizer.

Preparation time: 15 minutes
Cooking time: 15 minutes
Serves: 4–6

1	**whole chicken breast (2 halves), skinned and boned**
¾	**cup water**
1	**tablespoon lemon juice**
½	**cup chopped onion**
1	**teaspoon minced garlic**
1	**small hot pepper, minced, with seeds**
2	**tablespoons vegetable oil**
10–12	**tomatillos, husked and chopped fine**

Salt to taste
    ¼ **cup chopped fresh coriander (cilantro)**

1. Put chicken, water, and lemon juice into a small, nonstick skillet. Heat to simmer; cover and simmer about 6 minutes, until chicken is no longer pink and juices run clear. Strain (reserve broth for other use, if desired); cool. Dice.

2. Put onion, garlic, hot pepper, and oil in a 2-quart saucepan. Cook, stirring often, about 3 minutes, until onion softens.

3. Stir in tomatillos. Do not cover. Cook over medium-low heat about 5 minutes, until tender. Stir in chicken, salt, and coriander. Serve warm or at room temperature.

CHICKEN AND SHRIMP KABOBS

Chicken chunks are marinated to pick up a sweet, ginger-spiked flavor, then teamed with fresh shrimp and pineapple tidbits for a tasty, finger-food appetizer. The chicken can be marinated and the shrimp cleaned hours before guests arrive.

Preparation time: 15 minutes
Marinating time: 30 minutes
Cooking time: 5 minutes
Serves: 6–8

1 **8-ounce can pineapple chunks, in natural juices, or about 20 fresh pineapple chunks, plus ¼ cup orange juice**
2 **tablespoons vegetable oil**
1 **tablespoon lemon juice**
1 **teaspoon soy sauce**
1 **teaspoon minced fresh ginger**
3 **dashes hot pepper sauce**
1 **whole chicken breast (2 halves), skinned, boned, and cubed**
20 **medium (21–25 count) shrimp, shelled and deveined**
Coriander (cilantro) sprigs, for garnish

1. If using canned pineapple, drain ¼ cup pineapple juice into a medium bowl. If using fresh pineapple, use ¼ cup orange juice. Set aside pineapple chunks. Stir in oil, lemon juice, soy sauce, ginger, hot pepper sauce, and chicken cubes. Stir to coat well. Cover and refrigerate 20–30 minutes.

2. Mix in shrimp and let stand 5–10 minutes. Skewer a piece of chicken, a chunk of pineapple, and a shrimp onto each toothpick or short bamboo skewer. Put onto greased broiler pan. Broil 4 inches from heat source, 4–5 minutes, until centers of chicken pieces are no longer pink and shrimp have just turned pink, turning once.

MICROWAVE OVEN METHOD—6 minutes: Follow Step 1 and make skewers in Step 2. *Arrange skewers or toothpicks six to eight at a time in a spokelike fashion on a large plate, with shrimp ends toward the center. Cover with plastic wrap, vented. MICROWAVE (high) 1½–2 minutes, until centers of chicken pieces are no longer pink and shrimp have just turned pink. Repeat with remaining skewers. Drain and serve.*

TIP: Soak wooden picks or bamboo skewers in water to cover for about 20 minutes before using to prevent burning.

CHICKEN RUMAKI

Bacon-wrapped chicken bits make a tasty, high-protein finger food that is ideal for cocktail parties because you can make them hours ahead—or even freeze them.

Just the smell of cooking bacon gets the appetite juices rolling, so count on guests eating at least three rumaki each.

Preparation time: 15 minutes
Cooking time: 4–6 minutes
Serves: 6–8

1 whole chicken breast (2 halves), skinned, boned
8 strips bacon
¼ cup honey-mustard, plum sauce, or hoisin sauce
2 tablespoons minced fresh parsley

1. Cut chicken into 1-inch pieces. Cut bacon strips into thirds. Brush each bacon piece with honey-mustard or sauce. Wrap each chicken piece in bacon and secure with a wooden toothpick.
2. Arrange wrapped chicken pieces, 12 at a time, on broiler pan. Broil, 4 inches from heat source, 4–6 minutes, until bacon is crisp, turning often. Drizzle on a little more sauce, if desired. Sprinkle with parsley. Serve while hot.

MICROWAVE OVEN METHOD—8 minutes: Follow Step 1. Then arrange wrapped chicken pieces, 12 at a time, around the edges of a paper-towel-lined plate. For best crisping, do not let pieces touch. Cover with another paper towel. MICROWAVE (high) 4–5 minutes, until crisp. Complete with more sauce and parsley. Repeat with remaining rumaki. If frozen, microwave rumaki an extra 1 or 2 minutes, until crisp.

TIP: Do not walk away when broiling rumaki—they burn easily.

CHICKEN LIVER PATE

I love chicken liver pâté. And I especially love it when I can make this fine appetizer with "free" livers stashed away from other chicken meals. Serve from an attractive bowl or crock with bagel chips or crusty bread.

Preparation time: 15 minutes
Cooking time: 10 minutes
Chilling time: overnight
Serves: 6–8

¼ cup minced onion
1 teaspoon minced garlic
6 tablespoons butter or margarine
2 tablespoons Cognac or brandy
1 pound chicken livers, cut in half
3 sprigs parsley
2 teaspoons fresh thyme *or* ½ teaspoon dried
¼ teaspoon salt or to taste
⅛ teaspoon freshly ground black pepper

1. Put onion, garlic, and 4 tablespoons of the butter in a large, nonstick skillet. Cook and stir over medium heat about 3 minutes, until onion is tender.
2. Stir in Cognac and chicken livers. Cook 5–6 minutes, until liver centers are no longer pink, stirring frequently.
3. Put parsley in food processor and process until fine. Add liver mixture, thyme, salt, and pepper. Process until smooth. Cut up remaining 2 tablespoons butter and add to processor. Process briefly until just smooth. Spoon into bowl or crock, cover with plastic wrap, and chill in refrigerator for several hours or, preferably, overnight. Before serving, let stand at room temperature 20 minutes.

SESAME CHICKEN WINGS

Whole-wheat bread crumbs help add color to these appetizer wings. The wings can be cooked ahead, then kept in the refrigerator or freezer.

Preparation time: 20 minutes
Cooking time: 20–25 minutes
Serves: 4–6

10 chicken wings (2 pounds)
1 cup dry, whole-wheat bread crumbs (see Tip)
¼ cup chopped fresh parsley
¼ cup sesame seeds
½ teaspoon chili powder
1 teaspoon salt
¼ teaspoon freshly ground black pepper
4 tablespoons butter
1 tablespoon lemon juice
¼ teaspoon dry mustard
¼ teaspoon ground ginger
Dash cayenne

1. Heat oven to 375°F. Cut tips from chicken wings and discard. Cut chicken wings at joint, making two pieces from each wing. Set aside.
2. Mix bread crumbs, parsley, sesame seeds, chili powder, salt, and pepper in a shallow bowl. Melt butter in a small saucepan (or MICROWAVE on high for 1 minute in a small bowl). Stir lemon juice, dry mustard, ginger, and cayenne into butter.
3. Dip wings in butter mixture then bread-crumb mixture, patting to help crumbs stick. Arrange wings on a shallow, nonstick baking pan (a broiler-pan bottom lined with foil works well). Bake for 20–25 minutes, until meat is no longer pink in the center and the juices run clear.

TIP: To make bread crumbs, toast whole-wheat bread, then process in food processor. Four slices make about 1 cup crumbs.

TIP: To store cooked and cooled wings, wrap in waxed-paper layers, then foil, and keep in the refrigerator for 2 days or the freezer for 2 weeks. To reheat, bake in a 375°F oven for 10 minutes, or arrange on a plate in spokelike fashion and MICROWAVE on medium power 3–4 minutes, until heated through.

SOUPS

A big bowl of homemade chicken soup is the ultimate comfort food, whether it's traditional, Old-Fashioned Chicken-Vegetable Soup or a more exotic Tortilla-Lime Soup. And if you're an avid chicken cook, it's an economical use for those extra necks, wings, and other unused bones.

Scratch soups do need time to develop flavor, so most of the recipes here will keep your kitchen filled with a wonderful aroma for a couple of hours. If you're in a hurry, however, you can turn to Chicken and Shrimp Broth or Japanese Noodle Soup for ways to doctor up good-quality canned broth for a quick meal.

BASIC CHICKEN STOCK

A roasting chicken will give a deeper flavor, but a fine stock can be made with a simple fryer. Add all the skin, plus any extra skins that you may have removed and frozen. They contribute extra flavor, and the fat from the skin is easy to remove after the stock is refrigerated.

I don't use livers for white stock; the flavor is much too strong. And I don't use chicken hearts either, because I find the flavor too beefy for a chicken stock.

Serve this basic stock in a big mug as a light snack, or use as an ingredient in soups and other recipes.

Preparation time: 15 minutes
Cooking time: 2 hours
Yield: about 6 cups

1 **3-pound chicken, or 3 pounds chicken parts or meaty chicken or veal bones**
1 **coarsely chopped carrot**
1 **small onion, quartered**
2 **coarsely chopped celery ribs with fresh yellow leaves**
¼ **cup chopped fresh parsley**
1 **bay leaf, crushed**
6 **peppercorns**
1 **teaspoon fresh thyme** *or* ¼ **teaspoon dried**
8 **cups water**
½ **teaspoon salt (optional)**

1. Put all ingredients except salt in a 4-quart Dutch oven or stockpot. Bring to a boil; skim off and discard foam. Reduce heat and simmer, partially covered, 1½–2 hours, until chicken is tender.
2. Strain. Use a large spoon to skim off fat. Or, if you have time, first refrigerate the stock to make it easier to remove all the fat. Add salt as desired.

TIP: Pick the meat off the bones and save for soups, sandwiches, or salads.

TIP: Refrigerate, covered, up to a week, or freeze up to 3 months.

CHEAP CHICKEN SOUP

If you bone your own chicken breasts, and save the bones in the freezer, it doesn't take long to accumulate enough for a couple of bowls of cheap chicken soup—made for the cost of a little salt and pepper, plus some leftover spaghetti or rice.

Preparation time: 5 minutes
Cooking time: 1 hour
Serves: 4

3 pounds chicken bones with some meat attached, and skin
1 teaspoon salt
⅛ teaspoon freshly ground black pepper
6 cups water
1 cup leftover cooked rice or pasta

1. Put chicken bones and skin, salt, pepper, and water in a 4-quart Dutch oven or stockpot. Bring to a boil; skim off and discard foam. Reduce heat and simmer, partially covered, 1½–2 hours. Strain. Pick any meat from bones and return meat to pot. Discard bones and skin.
2. Use a large spoon to skim off fat. Or, if you have time, first refrigerate the stock to make it easier to remove all the fat.
3. Return stock to pot. Stir in rice or pasta. Reheat and serve.

TIP: *Don't be tempted to add too much water or the broth will be too thin. If you do err, add a teaspoon of a good chicken base (there are some on the market made without monosodium glutamate or excessive salt).*

TIP: *For a more substantial soup, add leftover chopped chicken or cooked vegetables.*

CHICKEN AND SHRIMP BROTH

This simple, light soup from the microwave oven features moist, tender chicken and succulent shrimp. Slender strips of fresh pea pods provide pretty color and a contrasting crunch. This healthful soup is fast, too—most of the cooking time is needed simply to heat the stock.

Preparation time: 10 minutes
Microwave time: 13 minutes
Serves: 4

4 **cups Basic Chicken Stock (see Index) or chicken broth**
½ **chicken breast (1 fillet), skinned, boned, and cut into ½-inch-wide strips**
8 **medium-sized shrimp, shelled and cleaned**
¼ **teaspoon sesame oil**
4 **Chinese pea pods, cut into very thin strips**

1. Put Basic Chicken Stock in a 2-quart casserole. Cover. MICROWAVE (high) 10–12 minutes, until boiling. Stir in chicken. Cover. MICROWAVE (high) 2–3 minutes, until centers of chicken pieces are no longer pink.
2. Stir in shrimp and sesame oil. Cover. MICROWAVE (high) 1–2 minutes, until shrimp are just pink. Ladle soup into bowls. Top with pea pods while soup is still hot and stir lightly.

JAPANESE NOODLE SOUP

Fresh ginger and a hot pepper are cooked first in sesame oil to develop flavor for this simple noodle soup made in the microwave oven. Plain ramen *noodles can be purchased in Oriental food marts; or, use a package of* ramen *soup and discard the overly salty, dry seasoning mix.*

Preparation time: 10 minutes
Microwave time: 16 minutes
Serves: 4

2 slices fresh ginger, cut into fine strips
1 small hot red pepper, cut into very thin, diagonal slices
½ teaspoon sesame oil
4 cups Basic Chicken Stock (see Index) or chicken broth
1 whole chicken breast (2 halves), skinned, boned, and cubed
1 3-ounce package *ramen* noodles (*chuja soba*)
2 green onions, white portion and first 2 inches of green, sliced thin

1. Put ginger, hot pepper, and oil in a 2½-quart casserole. Do not cover. MICROWAVE (high) about 1 minute, until vegetables are soft.
2. Stir in Basic Chicken Stock. Cover. MICROWAVE (high) 10–12 minutes, until boiling. Remove cover carefully. Stir in chicken. Cover. MICROWAVE (high) 3–4 minutes, until boiling.
3. Stir in noodles. Cover. MICROWAVE (high) 2–3 minutes, until chicken is no longer pink in the center and the noodles are soft. Stir in green onion.

CHICKEN-SPINACH SOUP

Fresh ginger imparts a lovely, Oriental flavor to the broth in this simple soup, which is loaded with fresh spinach. Most of the cooking time is needed to bring the broth to a boil; a few minutes more, and the soup is ready for the table.

Preparation time: 10 minutes
Cooking time: 15 minutes
Serves: 4

4 cups Basic Chicken Stock (see Index) or chicken broth
1 quarter-sized slice fresh ginger
1 whole chicken breast (2 halves), skinned, boned, and cubed
4 cups fresh spinach, rinsed well and cut into ½-inch strips
Sesame oil (optional)
2 green onions, white portion and first 2 inches of green, chopped

1. Put Basic Chicken Stock and ginger in a 2-quart saucepan. Heat to boil; reduce heat and simmer 5 minutes. Remove ginger.
2. Stir in chicken. Simmer 5 minutes, until centers of chicken pieces are no longer pink. Stir in spinach. Cook and stir about 5 minutes, until spinach wilts. Drizzle a drop or two of sesame oil over each serving, if desired. Sprinkle with green onions.

SPICY CHICKEN GAZPACHO

This colorful soup is chock-full of crisp vegetables—much like a gazpacho with chicken added. Serve it warm or cold.

Preparation time: 20 minutes
Cooking time: 20 minutes
Serves: 4

½ cup chopped onion
1 teaspoon minced garlic
1 tablespoon olive oil
1 whole chicken breast (2 halves), skinned, boned, and cut into ½-inch cubes
1 medium green bell pepper, cored, seeded, and minced
1 medium cucumber, peeled, seeded, and minced
2 medium tomatoes, peeled, seeded, and chopped
1½ cups (2 6-ounce cans) spicy tomato juice (such as V-8)
2 or 3 dashes crushed red pepper flakes
¼ teaspoon salt
⅛ teaspoon freshly ground black pepper
2 tablespoons minced fresh parsley or coriander (cilantro)
Dollops of plain yogurt (good when soup is served cold)

1. Put onion, garlic, and olive oil in a 3-quart, nonstick saucepan. Cook and stir 3 minutes to soften.
2. Stir in chicken. Cook and stir over medium-high heat 5 minutes, until centers of chicken pieces are no longer pink.
3. Stir in green pepper, cucumber, tomatoes, and ¼ cup of spicy tomato juice. Cook and stir over medium-high heat 5 minutes, until vegetables are just tender, stirring once. Stir in remaining tomato juice, red pepper flakes, salt, and pepper. Simmer 5 minutes to heat through. Taste and adjust seasonings. Sprinkle parsley or coriander atop each serving; if served cold, top with yogurt.

TIP: If serving cold, cook vegetables only 3 minutes to soften slightly. Complete recipe and chill in refrigerator for at least 2 hours, or overnight.

CHICKEN GUMBO

Okra stars as the flavorful glue in this slightly spicy, stick-to-the-ribs soup. Serve over hot, cooked rice.

Preparation time: 20 minutes
Cooking time: 50 minutes
Serves: 6–8

½ cup vegetable oil
½ cup flour
1 cup chopped onion
½ cup chopped celery
½ cup chopped green bell
   pepper
1½ teaspoons minced garlic
6 cups Basic Chicken Stock
   (see Index)
¼ teaspoon cayenne
1 teaspoon chopped fresh
   thyme *or* ¼ teaspoon dried
   thyme
½ teaspoon salt
¼ teaspoon freshly ground
   black pepper
1 whole chicken breast (2
   halves), skinned, boned, and
   cut into 1-inch cubes
4 small chicken thighs,
   skinned, boned, and cut into
   1-inch cubes
½ pound andouille or smoked
   Polish sausage, sliced thin
1½ cups sliced fresh or frozen
   okra, thawed
Hot pepper sauce

1. Heat oil in a 4-quart Dutch oven over medium-high heat until hot. Add flour; cook and stir constantly, about 5–10 minutes, until mixture is the color of cinnamon.
2. Stir in onion, celery, green pepper, and garlic. Cook and stir about 5 minutes. Stir in chicken broth and seasonings. Simmer 10 minutes, stirring often, until mixture thickens.
3. Stir in chicken; simmer 15 minutes until chicken is tender. Stir in sausage and okra. Simmer about 5 minutes, until okra is crisp-tender. Taste and adjust seasonings. Pass the hot pepper sauce.

TIP: Select small okra pods, 1½ to 2 inches long. The freshest and most tender have a velvetlike exterior. They can be stored for up to 2 days in the refrigerator, unwashed, dry, and loosely wrapped. Wash and slice just before cooking. Handle carefully, for okra bruises easily, blackening within a few hours.

CABBAGE DINNER SOUP

This lusty soup—loaded with healthful cabbage, carrots, kidney beans, tomatoes, and chicken thighs—makes an excellent dinner with some crusty French bread.

Preparation time: 25 minutes
Cooking time: 45 minutes
Serves: 6–8

4 slices bacon, cut into 1-inch pieces
4 chicken thighs, skinned, boned, and cut into 1-inch pieces
2 cups chopped onion
1 cup diced carrot
½ cup diced celery
¾ teaspoon dried thyme
1 tablespoon brown sugar
¼ teaspoon salt
½ teaspoon freshly ground black pepper
3 sprigs fresh parsley, chopped
1 bay leaf
Dash ground cloves
6 cups Basic Chicken Stock (see Index) or chicken broth
1 28-ounce can tomatoes, with juice
1 large head cabbage (4 pounds), chopped coarse (about 7 cups)
1 15½-ounce can kidney beans, drained
1 tablespoon cider vinegar
Sour cream (optional)

1. Place bacon in a 4-quart Dutch oven. Cook and stir over medium heat 3–4 minutes, until crisp. Use a slotted spoon to remove bacon, leaving fat in the casserole. Drain bacon on paper towels. Crumble and reserve.
2. Sauté chicken 3 minutes in bacon fat; remove. Stir in onion, carrot, celery, thyme, brown sugar, salt, and pepper. Cook and stir 3 minutes, until partially cooked.
3. Add parsley, bay leaf, cloves, Basic Chicken Stock, and tomatoes. Heat to boil; reduce heat and stir in cabbage. Cook partially covered 30 minutes until cabbage is softened as desired. Stir in beans. Stir in vinegar. Heat through. Serve sprinkled with bacon and, if desired, a dollop of sour cream.

TIP: Keep bacon in the freezer. To defrost, pull back plastic wrap to expose the number of slices desired. Wrap the rest in aluminum foil. Place in the microwave oven at least 1 inch away from the walls. Defrost on the defrost cycle or low power. The part protected by foil will remain frozen. Remove desired slices. Return the rest of the bacon to the freezer.

OLD-FASHIONED CHICKEN-VEGETABLE SOUP

This recipe takes some time and fussing, but the result is a huge bowlful of super-healthful soup. Note that the more dense, slower-cooking vegetables such as carrots and celery are added first; fast-cooking vegetables such as corn and tomatoes are added at the end.

Preparation time: 30 minutes
Cooking time: about 2 hours
Serves: 6

1 **3-pound fryer chicken, cut up**
3 **carrots**
3 **celery ribs with fresh yellow leaves**
1 **small turnip**
1 **small onion**
2 **large sprigs parsley**
1 **bay leaf, crushed**
6 **peppercorns**
1 **teaspoon fresh thyme** *or* ¼ **teaspoon dried**
8 **cups water**
1 **14-ounce can chicken broth**
1 **teaspoon salt**
½ **cup frozen corn**
1 **ripe tomato, seeded and chopped**
1 **cup cooked pasta or rice (optional)**

1. Remove chicken liver, heart, and gizzards from the chicken and save for some other use. Saving all ends and scraps, cut carrots and celery into ¼-inch-thick slices; peel and dice turnip; and chop onion. Reserve the cut pieces. Put the scraps in a 4-quart Dutch oven or stockpot.
2. Add the chicken, parsley, bay leaf, peppercorns, thyme, water, chicken broth, and salt to the pan. Cover tightly. Heat to boil over medium-high heat. Skim off and discard foam. Turn over or rearrange chicken.
3. Simmer, partially covered, 1–1½ hours. Strain. Use a large spoon to skim off fat. Or, if you have time, first refrigerate the stock to make it easier to remove all the fat. Remove skin and bones from chicken; cut meat into bite-sized pieces and reserve.
4. Stir in trimmed and cut carrots, celery, turnip, and onion. Cook, covered, over medium heat 20–25 minutes, until vegetables are tender. Stir in corn, tomato, pasta or rice, and cooked chicken meat. Simmer about 5 minutes, until heated through.

TIP: Keep the carrot slices thin; they require the longest cooking time of any of the vegetables.

TIP: The whole fryer yields about 3 cups of cooked meat, which is quite a bit for soup. You may want to reserve a cup for other uses such as salads.

PEASANT SOUP

Don't balk at the two heads of garlic—they mellow when they cook and give this soup a wonderfully hearty flavor. This soup takes advantage of legs and thighs, which are less expensive than chicken breasts. However, any chicken parts could be used. Serve with thick slices of crusty bread and steins of beer.

Preparation time: 15 minutes
Cooking time: 45 minutes
Serves: 4

2 heads (30 cloves) garlic, peeled (see Tip) and crushed
¼ cup minced onion
2 tablespoons butter
2 cups grated potato (about 2 medium)
1 carrot, grated
2 cups Basic Chicken Stock (see Index) or chicken broth
⅛ teaspoon freshly ground black pepper
2 chicken legs and thighs, split and skinned
Chopped fresh parsley

1. Put garlic, onion, and butter in a 3-quart saucepan. Sauté 3–5 minutes, until tender. Add potato and carrot. Cook, covered, over low heat 10 minutes, until potato and carrot are tender, stirring occasionally. Add Basic Chicken Stock. Puree in blender or processor.
2. Return soup to casserole. Stir in pepper and chicken. Simmer, partially covered, 30–40 minutes, until chicken juices no longer run pink when chicken is pricked. Remove bones from chicken. Pull meat into shreds and return to soup. Sprinkle parsley over soup before serving.

TIP: Use this great microwave technique to peel garlic, whether the garlic is intended for a microwave or conventional cooking recipe:

Put the whole head of garlic in the microwave oven. MICROWAVE (high) 45 seconds, turning the head upside down after half the time. Let stand 1 minute to cool. Squeeze the papery skin, and the garlic cloves will pop out.

For individual cloves, put them on a paper towel or plate. MICROWAVE (high) 30 seconds. Let stand and remove skins as above.

TORTILLA-LIME SOUP

This soup, which we first encountered in Mérida, the Yucatán capital of Mexico, is a riotously colorful dish filled with strips of crisp tortillas. For a good contrast in textures, be sure to serve the soup immediately after the tortillas and avocados are added.

Preparation time: 20 minutes
Cooking time: 20 minutes
Serves: 4

6 6-inch corn tortillas
Vegetable oil
1 teaspoon minced garlic
¼ cup minced onion
2 medium tomatoes, peeled, seeded, and chopped
¼ teaspoon ground cumin
½ teaspoon chili powder
1 bay leaf, broken in half
4 cups Basic Chicken Stock (see Index) or chicken broth
¼ teaspoon salt
Dash cayenne
1 whole chicken breast (2 halves), skinned, boned, and cubed
1 tablespoon lime juice
1 small avocado, peeled, seeded, and cubed
½ cup shredded cheddar
Chopped fresh coriander (cilantro)

1. Cut tortillas into ¾-inch strips. Pour vegetable oil into a large, nonstick skillet to depth of ⅛ inch. Heat over medium heat until hot but not smoking. Fry strips, a few at a time, about 30–35 seconds, until golden and crisp, turning often. Drain on paper towels.
2. Heat 1 tablespoon oil in a 2½-quart saucepan; add garlic, onion, and tomatoes. Sauté 3 minutes until onion is tender.
3. Stir in cumin, chili powder, bay leaf, Basic Chicken Stock, salt, and cayenne. Heat to boil over medium heat. Simmer 10 minutes.
4. Stir in chicken. Simmer 5 minutes, until centers of chicken pieces are no longer pink. Stir in lime juice and tortilla strips. Top with avocado and cheese; sprinkle with coriander. Serve immediately.

TIP: Don't substitute light-colored wheat tortillas for yellow-colored corn tortillas. The wheat ones will get limp and soggy.

SALADS

Chameleonlike chicken is ideal as the main protein in a salad. Mix it with raspberry vinaigrette and its subtle taste goes upscale. Toss in plenty of mayonnaise (with a touch of chopped pickle) and you have the start of an all-American-favorite chicken salad.

Because boneless chicken breasts cook so quickly you don't have to wait for leftover chicken to make a chicken salad. A couple of chicken breasts take only a few minutes to cook—just enough time to whip together fresh vegetables and greens for a warm chicken salad entree.

Or use your microwave oven to cook one or more of the salad ingredients—like asparagus in the Chicken-Asparagus Salad—on the same plate with the chicken. The total cooking time is 3 minutes. One hour later, your salad is chilled and ready to eat.

RASPBERRY-CHICKEN SALAD

Still-warm chicken is tossed in raspberry vinaigrette, then left to chill and marinate. Fresh raspberries and banana—a great taste combination—are teamed up with fresh mint for the final presentation. Serve for lunch or a light summer dinner.

Preparation time: 10 minutes
Cooking time: 6 minutes
Chilling time: 2 hours
Serves: 2–4

**2 whole chicken breasts
(4 halves), skinned and boned
1 cup water
2 tablespoons fresh lemon juice
2 tablespoons raspberry vinegar
3 tablespoons vegetable oil
1 teaspoon honey
¼ teaspoon almond extract
1 small head Bibb lettuce
1 ripe banana
½ cup fresh raspberries
2 tablespoons chopped fresh
mint**

1. Put chicken, water, and 1 tablespoon of lemon juice in a large, nonstick skillet. Heat to simmer; cover and continue simmering, about 6 minutes, until chicken is no longer pink and juices run clear. Strain. (Reserve broth for other use, if desired.) Cut chicken into 1-inch cubes.
2. Whisk remaining 1 tablespoon lemon juice, vinegar, oil, honey, and almond extract in a small bowl. Pour over warm chicken and turn chicken several times to coat. Cover chicken and chill in refrigerator 2–6 hours.
3. To serve, arrange lettuce leaves on a plate. Toss chicken in vinaigrette and place on top of lettuce. Peel banana, cut into diagonal slices, and arrange among chicken. Scatter raspberries on plate. Sprinkle with mint.

TIP: 4 cups of cubed, cooked, leftover chicken may be substituted.

CHICKEN-ASPARAGUS SALAD

This light salad features simply cooked chicken and asparagus tossed with a tarragon-mustard vinaigrette. It's particularly easy to make using just one plate in a microwave oven, so those directions are given first. Serve warm or chilled.

Preparation time: 5 minutes
Microwave time: 8 minutes
Serves: 2–4

½ **pound asparagus, cut into 2-inch lengths**
1 **whole chicken breast (2 halves), skinned, boned, and cut into 1½- by ¼-inch strips**
1 **tablespoon white-wine vinegar**
1 **teaspoon fresh lemon juice**
1 **teaspoon Dijon mustard**
½ **teaspoon finely minced garlic**
1 **teaspoon chopped fresh tarragon *or* ¼ teaspoon dried**
⅛ **teaspoon salt**
⅛ **teaspoon freshly ground black pepper**
3 **tablespoons vegetable oil**
2 **green onions, white portion and first 2 inches of green, sliced**

1. Place asparagus in center of a plate. Arrange chicken around the edges. Cover with plastic wrap, vented. MICROWAVE (high) 3–4 minutes, until asparagus are tender-crisp and center of chicken is no longer pink, stirring chicken pieces once. Let stand 2 minutes. Drain. Cover and chill in refrigerator for at least 1 hour, if desired.
2. In a small bowl, whisk together vinegar, lemon juice, mustard, garlic, tarragon, salt, and pepper. Whisk in oil. Drizzle vinaigrette over asparagus and chicken and gently toss. Sprinkle with green onion.

CONVENTIONAL OVEN METHOD—8 minutes: (1) You will need an extra tablespoon of oil to stir-fry the chicken. Cook asparagus in a medium saucepan of boiling water 3 minutes, until crisp-tender. Drain. Heat 1 tablespoon oil in a large, nonstick skillet. Cook and stir chicken over medium-high heat 4–5 minutes, until no longer pink. Drain. Cover and chill in refrigerator for at least 1 hour, if desired. Follow Step 2.

CHICKEN-AVOCADO SALAD

Chicken cubes and orange segments are moistened with a lovely green avocado dressing.

Preparation time: 15 minutes
Cooking time: 35 minutes
Serves: 4

2 **whole chicken breasts (4 halves), split**
1 **ripe avocado**
1 **tablespoon lemon juice**
1 **tablespoon white-wine vinegar**
¼ **cup chopped fresh coriander (cilantro)**
¼ **cup mayonnaise**
¼ **teaspoon salt**
⅛ **teaspoon freshly ground black pepper**
4 **cups lettuce**
4 **oranges, sectioned**

1. Heat oven to 350°F. Put chicken in a nonstick baking pan. Bake 30–35 minutes, until juices run clear. Drain. Remove and discard skin and bones. Cube meat. Use immediately or cover and chill in refrigerator 2 hours or overnight.
2. In a small bowl, mash half of the avocado and the lemon juice, vinegar, coriander, mayonnaise, salt, and pepper.
3. On plates or a serving platter, arrange lettuce, orange sections, and chicken. Cut up remaining avocado and divide among the plates. Spoon avocado dressing over salad.

TIP: You may substitute 4 cups of cubed, leftover chicken.

MOM'S CHICKEN SALAD

Nothing ever beats Mom's chicken salad—and this is the way (as close as she could estimate) that my mom, Sophie Riess, makes this lunch special.

Instead of starting from scratch, you can, of course, use about 2 cups of leftover cooked chicken. This is a particularly fine way to use the meat left over from making chicken stock or soup.

Preparation time: 15 minutes
Cooking time: 30 minutes
Chilling time: overnight
Serves: 6

4 chicken thighs
2 whole chicken breasts
(4 halves)
¼ cup and 2 tablespoons mayonnaise
¼ cup and 2 tablespoons sour cream
¼ cup chopped sweet (sandwich) pickles
1 tablespoon fresh dill *or*
1 teaspoon dried
¼ cup minced green pepper
¾ to 1 teaspoon salt or to taste
¼ teaspoon freshly ground black pepper

1. Heat oven to 350°F. Put chicken thighs and breasts in a 13″ × 9″, nonstick baking pan. Bake for 30–35 minutes, until center of chicken is no longer pink and juices run clear. Drain and reserve juices for soups and sauces. Skin and bone chicken. Cut meat into ½-inch cubes.
2. Mix chicken, mayonnaise, sour cream, pickles, dill, green pepper, salt, and pepper in a medium-sized bowl. Cover and chill overnight in the refrigerator. Serve salad on a bun or on lettuce.

TIP: *Warm food absorbs flavors better. If using leftover chicken for this dish, first reheat (you can MICROWAVE on medium-low power 2–3 minutes), then add the rest of the ingredients and chill.*

APPLE-CHICKEN SALAD
WITH PEANUT DRESSING

This is a wonderfully satisfying salad, chock-full of crunchy peanuts and vegetables. The spicy version (see Tip) is especially appealing to adults.

Preparation time: 20 minutes
Cooking time: 35 minutes
Serves: 4

 2 **whole chicken breasts
    (4 halves), split**
¼ **cup chunky peanut butter**
¼ **cup honey**
½ **cup mayonnaise**
 1 **apple (Granny Smith is good),
    diced**
 1 **tablespoon lemon juice**
½ **cup golden raisins**
½ **cup diced celery**
 1 **cup chopped red cabbage**
Salt to taste
 8 **leaves red-tipped curly leaf
    lettuce**

1. Heat oven to 350°F. Put chicken into a baking pan. Bake 30–35 minutes, until center of chicken is no longer pink and the juices run clear. Remove and discard skin and bones. Cube meat. Use immediately or cover and chill in refrigerator for 2 hours or overnight.
2. In a medium-sized bowl, mix peanut butter, honey, and mayonnaise. Add chicken and mix well. Add apple, lemon juice, raisins, celery, cabbage, and salt. Toss until mixed.
3. To serve, arrange lettuce leaves on plates or a platter. Spoon chicken mixture on top.

TIP: *For a spicy version, add 6–10 drops hot pepper sauce, such as Tabasco, to the peanut butter mixture before adding the chicken.*

TIP: *You may substitute 4 cups cubed, leftover chicken.*

CHICKEN-CHAYOTE SALAD

Team leftover chicken with freshly cooked chayote, a pear-shaped gourd popular in Mexico and South America and increasingly available in supermarkets here. A chayote is crisp like an apple and tastes like a cross between a cucumber and a zucchini—a nice match with chicken.

Preparation time: 10 minutes
Cooking time: 5 minutes
Chilling time: 2 hours
Serves: 4

2 chayote, pared, cored, and cut into ¼-inch cubes (2 cups)
½ cup mayonnaise
1 tablespoon Dijon mustard
¼ teaspoon salt
⅛ teaspoon freshly ground black pepper
2 green onions, white portion and first 2 inches of green, sliced
2 cups cooked, skinless, cubed chicken breast
½ cup dry-roasted peanuts

1. Put chayote into a 2-quart saucepan with water to cover. Heat to boil. Cook, 3–5 minutes, until crisp-tender. Drain.
2. In a 2-quart bowl, blend mayonnaise, mustard, salt, and pepper. Mix in green onion, chicken, peanuts, and cooked chayote. Cover. Refrigerate for 2 hours to blend flavors.

TIP: To cube fresh chayote, first cut off thin slices from both bumpy ends. Discard ends. Cut rest in half lengthwise. Peel as you would an apple.

Use a serrated tool (a grapefruit spoon works well) or melon baller to remove white, pithy core and almond-shaped seed. Reserve edible seed. Discard core.

Turn chayote halves flat side down on a cutting board. Cut into slices or cubes.

TIP: Chayote seed has an extraordinary taste, much like a fresh nut just off a tree. If you're impatient, munch it raw. But the flavor deepens when the seed is cooked. Slip it into a dish for the last 2 minutes to cook.

MACADAMIA-CHICKEN SALAD

Tender chicken breasts are marinated, cooked, and chilled in pineapple juice until juicy-tender, then served with pineapple chunks, crushed macadamia nuts, and fresh mint. A wonderful salad!

Preparation time: 10 minutes
Marinating time: 10 minutes
Cooking time: 5 minutes
Chilling time: 2 hours
Serves: 4

1 **whole chicken breast (2 halves), skinned, boned, and cut into ½-inch-wide strips**
1 **15-ounce can pineapple chunks in natural juices**
1 **head Bibb lettuce, rinsed and patted dry**
2½ **ounces (½ cup) macadamia nuts, lightly crushed**
Fresh mint leaves

1. Put chicken in a medium-sized, nonstick skillet. Pour ⅓ cup of the pineapple juices over the chicken and let marinate 10 minutes. Reserve the pineapple chunks.
2. Heat chicken to a simmer; cook, covered, over low heat, 4–5 minutes, until centers of chicken pieces are no longer pink. Drain.
3. To serve, arrange lettuce, chicken, and reserved pineapple chunks on a platter. Sprinkle with nuts. Garnish with mint.

TIP: Do not leave chicken in pineapple juice more than a few hours or the texture will become mushy. Do not use an aluminum pan.

SPICY CHICKEN AND SHRIMP SALAD

Chicken and shrimp are cooked in the same skillet, then tossed with hot spices. A touch of blue cheese helps counteract the spices.

Preparation time: 20 minutes
Cooking time: 5 minutes
Serves: 4

1 tablespoon vegetable oil
1 whole chicken breast (2 halves), skinned, boned, and cut into ½-inch-wide strips
½ pound raw, medium-sized shrimp, shelled and deveined
2 tablespoons lemon juice
¼ teaspoon cayenne
4–5 drops Tabasco or other hot pepper sauce
2 tablespoons minced fresh parsley
½ teaspoon salt
¼ teaspoon freshly ground black pepper
4 cups assorted leaf lettuce
3 tablespoons olive oil
1 tablespoon white-wine vinegar
1 large ripe tomato, diced
2 ounces blue cheese, crumbled

1. Heat oil in a large, nonstick skillet until hot. Add chicken; cook and stir over medium heat 2 minutes. Add shrimp; cook and stir 2–3 minutes, until chicken pieces are no longer pink in the center and the shrimp have just turned pink. Remove from heat to a bowl.
2. In a small bowl, mix lemon juice, cayenne, Tabasco, parsley, salt, and half the pepper (⅛ teaspoon). Add to chicken and shrimp and toss well.
3. Put lettuce in a salad bowl or on a platter. Toss with olive oil, vinegar, and remaining pepper. Toss in chicken, shrimp, and tomato. Sprinkle with blue cheese. Serve immediately.

MICROWAVE OVEN METHOD—3 minutes: (1) Eliminate the 1 tablespoon oil. Place chicken along rim of a plate. Arrange shrimp in a circle in the center, tails pointing in. Cover with plastic wrap, vented. MICROWAVE (high) 3–4 minutes, until the centers of chicken pieces are no longer pink and shrimp have just turned pink. Drain. (2) Follow Steps 2 and 3.

WILD MUSHROOM-CHICKEN SALAD

Don't let the length of this recipe discourage you. The wild mushroom dressing can be made days ahead, and the chicken one day ahead, then assembled with fresh salad ingredients for an elegant salad entree. Dried porcini mushrooms can be found in Italian or other specialty food stores. Dried shiitake mushrooms, found in Oriental specialty stores, may be substituted.

Preparation time: 30 minutes
Soaking time: 10 minutes
Cooking time: 10 minutes
Serves: 4

2 **whole chicken breasts (4 halves), skinned and boned**
1 **cup water**
1 **tablespoon lemon juice**
¼ **cup (½ ounce) dried porcini mushrooms**
½ **cup red-wine vinegar**
¼ **cup diced sweet red bell pepper**
1 **small onion, sliced thin**
½ **cup olive oil, preferably extra-virgin**
1 **tablespoon chopped fresh tarragon** *or* ½ **teaspoon dried**
¼ **teaspoon salt**
⅛ **teaspoon freshly ground black pepper**
2 **cups Bibb lettuce**
1 **cup (lightly packed) fresh watercress leaves and stems**
1 **cup thinly sliced Belgian endive**
½ **pound button mushrooms, sliced**
4 **ripe plum tomatoes, cubed**

1. Put chicken, water, and lemon juice in a large, nonstick skillet. Heat to simmer; cover and simmer, about 6 minutes, until center of chicken is no longer pink and the juices run clear. Strain. (Reserve the broth for other uses, if desired.) Let chicken cool slightly, then cut into 1½-inch cubes. (Chicken may be made a day ahead and kept chilled in refrigerator.)

2. To make dressing, put dried mushrooms and vinegar in a small saucepan. Heat to boil over medium-low heat. Remove from heat. Let stand, covered, 10 minutes to soak.

3. Put red pepper, onion, and olive oil in a small, nonstick skillet. Cook and stir over medium-low heat 2 minutes, until softened.

4. Drain mushrooms through a water-soaked cheesecloth or coffee filter, reserving liquid. Rinse mushrooms briefly under cold water to remove grit. Trim and discard tough ends from mushrooms; chop mushrooms. Add chopped mushrooms, reserved liquid, tarragon, salt, and pepper to red pepper mixture. Whisk well with fork. (Dressing can be made ahead and stored for up to a week in the refrigerator.)

5. To assemble salad, arrange Bibb lettuce and watercress on serving plates. Top with chicken. Arrange Belgian endive, button mushrooms, and cubed tomatoes on salads. Drizzle with wild mushroom dressing.

TIP: You may substitute 4 cups cubed, leftover chicken.

CHICKEN NIÇOISE SALAD

I love this version of Niçoise salad—all the Mediterranean goodies plus chicken instead of tuna.

Preparation time: 15 minutes
Cooking time: 25 minutes
Chilling time: 2 hours
Serves: 4

2 whole chicken breasts (4 halves), skinned and boned
1 tablespoon lemon juice
1 cup water
2 cups green beans, cut into 1½-inch pieces
2 cups ¼-inch-sliced red potatoes with skins on
½ cup pitted black olives, preferably Mediterranean-style
6 tablespoons olive oil
¼ teaspoon dry mustard
2 tablespoons white-wine vinegar
½ teaspoon salt
2 medium tomatoes, quartered
6 thin slices Bermuda onion, separated into rings
16 large leaves red leaf lettuce
1 hard-boiled egg, peeled and quartered
8 anchovy fillets, drained
2 tablespoons chopped fresh tarragon *or* 1 teaspoon dried

1. Put chicken, lemon juice, and 1 cup water into a large, nonstick skillet. Heat to simmer; cover and continue simmering, about 6 minutes, until chicken is no longer pink in the center and the juices run clear. Strain. (Reserve juices for other use, if desired.) Cover chicken and chill in refrigerator at least 2 hours. Cut into 1½-inch cubes. (Chicken may be made a day ahead and kept chilled in refrigerator.)
2. Cook the beans in a medium-sized saucepan of boiling water, 6–7 minutes, until crisp-tender. Drain.
3. Cook the potatoes in a medium-sized saucepan of boiling water, 8–10 minutes, until fork-tender but not overcooked. Drain.
4. Mix olives, olive oil, mustard, vinegar, and salt in a large bowl. Mix in beans and potatoes. Cover. Refrigerate at least 2 hours.
5. Add tomato, onion, and cooked chicken. Toss gently to mix. Arrange lettuce on plates. Arrange chicken-and-vegetable mixture on top of lettuce. Add egg, top with criss-crossed anchovies, and sprinkle with tarragon.

MICROWAVE OVEN METHOD—12 minutes: (1) Arrange chicken on a plate, with thickest portions to the outside. Drizzle with lemon juice. Cover with plastic wrap, vented. MICROWAVE (high) 4–6 minutes, until chicken is no longer pink in the center, turning pieces over once. Drain. Follow rest of Step 1. (2) Put beans and ¼ cup water in a 2½-quart casserole. Cover. MICROWAVE (high) 2–3 minutes to give them a head start cooking. Stir in potatoes. Cover. MICROWAVE (high) 6–8 minutes, until just tender. Drain. Return to casserole. (3) Follow Steps 4 and 5.

TIP: *You may substitute 4 cups cubed, leftover chicken.*

MANGO-CHUTNEY CHICKEN SALAD

Fresh homemade mango chutney is a snap to prepare in the microwave oven and provides the base for a luscious summer salad. Serve with a chilled rice salad.

Preparation time: 30 minutes
Microwave time: 14 minutes
Chilling time: 2 hours
Serves: 4

4 chicken thighs
2 ripe mangoes
¼ cup minced onion
1 teaspoon minced fresh garlic
2 teaspoons minced fresh ginger
½ cup lightly packed brown sugar
1 small tomato, peeled, seeded, and chopped fine
½ cup walnuts, chopped fine
1 teaspoon mustard seeds
½ teaspoon ground cinnamon
⅛ teaspoon ground clove
⅛ teaspoon cayenne
2 tablespoons fresh lime juice

1. Put thighs on a plate with thickest portions to the outside. Cover with plastic wrap, vented. MICROWAVE (high) 7–9 minutes, until juices run clear, turning pieces over once. Drain. Set aside.

2. Peel mangoes, remove seeds, and chop remaining flesh. Mix onion, garlic, ginger, brown sugar, tomato, walnuts, mustard seeds, cinnamon, clove, and cayenne in a 2½-quart casserole. Cover with waxed paper. MICROWAVE (high) 2–3 minutes, until quite hot. Stir.

3. MICROWAVE (high), uncovered, 5–7 minutes, until fruit is soft. Stir in lime juice.

4. Remove skin and bones from chicken thighs and chop meat. Add to mango chutney. Stir well. Cover and chill in refrigerator at least 2 hours.

TURKEY-RICE SALAD

Leftover turkey reigns in this colorful, crunchy dinner salad. For instructions on how to cook a turkey breast, see Index.

Preparation time: 20 minutes
Cooking time: 20 minutes
Chilling time: 3 hours or overnight
Serves: 6–8

1 cup uncooked, long-grain rice
1 large ripe tomato, seeded and diced
1 cucumber, seeded and diced
1 green bell pepper, seeded, cored, and diced
1 16-ounce can chickpeas, rinsed and drained
1 6-ounce can pitted black olives, drained
2 cups cooked, diced turkey meat
½ cup diced red onion
½ cup olive oil
2 tablespoons lemon juice
1 tablespoon white-wine vinegar
3 tablespoons chopped fresh basil *or* 1 tablespoon dried
¼ cup minced fresh parsley
½ teaspoon salt
⅛ teaspoon freshly ground black pepper

1. Cook rice according to package directions.
2. Put cooked rice in a large bowl. Add tomato, cucumber, green pepper, chickpeas, olives, turkey, and onion. In a small bowl, whisk together olive oil, lemon juice, vinegar, basil, parsley, salt, and pepper. Toss into salad. Cover and chill in refrigerator 3 hours or overnight.

MICROWAVE OVEN METHOD—17 Minutes: (1) Mix rice, 2 cups water, and 1 teaspoon salt in a 2½-quart casserole. Cover. MICROWAVE (high) 5–7 minutes to boiling. MICROWAVE (medium) 12–14 minutes, until water is absorbed. (2) Follow Step 2.

QUICK PICKS

The trick to preparing a successful quick dish is to keep it simple—but keep it special. It takes only a few moments to add a little mustard, or a touch of lemon-chive or orange juice, and turn a plain chicken breast into a tasty dish.

Boned chicken breasts are particularly fast and easy to cook. Because these convenient cuts are so popular, they also are the most expensive part of the chicken. If you tend to do a lot of quick cooking, you may find it worth the time to buy split breasts on sale, bone and skin them yourself, and keep a supply wrapped in the freezer, ready to go.

For a particularly fast and more complete meal, put some vegetables and chicken on the same plate and cook them at the same time in the microwave oven. (Some vegetables cook quicker than others. I've included a list of these vegetables with the recipe for One-Plate Chicken and Vegetables.)

For other fast dishes, try Chicken and Shrimp Broth, Japanese Noodle Soup, Raspberry-Chicken Salad, Chicken-Asparagus Salad, Passion Fruit Chicken, and many of the recipes in the "Light Fare" and "Kid Stuff" chapters.

MOZZARELLA CHICKEN

This dish will be as good as the ingredients, so for best results use fresh basil leaves, a nice ripe tomato, and good-quality olive oil and cheese. Note that before the toppings are added, the chicken is first cooked thoroughly to ensure doneness.

Preparation time: 10 minutes
Cooking time: 9 minutes
Serves: 4

2 whole chicken breasts (4 halves), skinned and boned **10 fresh, large basil leaves *or* 1 teaspoon dried** **1 large, ripe tomato, sliced thin** **Salt** **Pepper** **1 teaspoon olive oil** **3 ounces mozzarella, grated**	1. Heat broiler to high. Put chicken between pieces of waxed paper and pound to ¼-inch thick. Put chicken on an oiled broiler pan. Broil, 4 inches from the heat, 6–8 minutes, until golden and juices run clear. 2. Chop two of the basil leaves and reserve. Arrange remaining ingredients on each chicken breast in this order: 2 basil leaves, overlapping tomato slices, salt, pepper, olive oil, and cheese. Broil, 4–6 inches from heat, 30–60 seconds, until cheese is golden. Sprinkle with chopped basil leaves and serve warm.

MICROWAVE OVEN METHOD—6 minutes: (1) Put chicken between pieces of waxed paper and pound to ¼ inch thick. Arrange chicken breasts around a plate, thickest portions to the outside. Cover with plastic wrap, vented. MICROWAVE (high) 4–6 minutes, until chicken is no longer pink in the center, turning pieces once. (2) Chop basil and arrange as in Step 2. MICROWAVE (medium) 2–3 minutes, until cheese melts. Sprinkle with chopped basil leaves and serve warm.

TIP: Although chicken breasts cook well in the microwave oven on high power, cheese is cooked on medium power to keep it from toughening.

SMASHED GARLIC CHICKEN

Just two extra ingredients—a head of garlic and some freshly ground black pepper—transform plain chicken into a tasty treat. Don't be alarmed by the amount of garlic; cooked garlic mellows into mild, nutty-flavored cloves which are smashed and scattered on top of the chicken. A little trick with the microwave oven greatly shortens the time and fuss needed to peel the garlic. The microwave recipe for this dish is so wonderfully short that it is offered first, with conventional cooking directions second.

Preparation time: 10 minutes
Microwave time: 5 minutes
Serves: 4

1 whole head garlic
2 whole chicken breasts
   (4 halves), skinned and boned
¼ teaspoon salt
Freshly ground black pepper

1. Put the whole head of garlic in the microwave oven. MICROWAVE (high) 35–50 seconds, turning the head upside down after half the time. Let stand 1 minute to cool. Squeeze the papery skin and let the garlic cloves pop out. Use the broad side of a knife or the back of a spoon to smash the cloves gently.
2. Arrange chicken on a plate with thickest portions to the outside. Scatter smashed garlic on top of the chicken. Cover with plastic wrap, vented. MICROWAVE (high) 4–6 minutes, until center of chicken is no longer pink, turning pieces over after 2 minutes. Before serving, rearrange garlic on top of chicken. Sprinkle with salt and pepper.

CONVENTIONAL OVEN METHOD—35 minutes: (1) Heat oven to 325°F. Boil garlic in a small saucepan of boiling water about 7 minutes, until tender. Drain. Squeeze the papery skin and let the garlic cloves pop out. Use the broad side of a knife or the back of a spoon to smash the cloves gently. (2) Put chicken in a single layer into a baking dish that has been generously oiled with olive oil. Top with garlic. Bake, tightly covered, 25 minutes, until center of chicken is no longer pink. Before serving, rearrange garlic on top of chicken. Sprinkle with salt and pepper.

COUNTRY-MUSTARD DRUMSTICKS

A smear of country-style mustard adds a pleasant zip to just-cooked chicken. This quick microwave recipe can be made with other chicken parts. (Check the Microwave Chicken Cooking Chart [see Index] for cooking times.)

Preparation time: 5 minutes
Microwave time: 6 minutes
Serves: 4

8 chicken drumsticks, skinned
4 tablespoons country-style
mustard

Arrange drumsticks on a plate in a spokelike fashion, meaty sides out, bone ends pointing in. Cover with plastic wrap, vented. MICROWAVE (high) 6–8 minutes, until meat is no longer pink, turning pieces over once. Drain. Let stand 2 minutes. Brush with mustard. Serve.

CONVENTIONAL OVEN METHOD—50 minutes: Heat oven to 325°F. Generously coat drumsticks on all sides with mustard. Put into a nonstick baking pan (or oiled regular pan). Bake 50 minutes, until juices run clear.

TIP: Any flavor mustard—such as honey-mustard or herb mustards—will work here.

TIP: For more punch, sprinkle mustard-coated chicken with freshly ground black pepper.

FENNEL SEED CHICKEN

This recipe demonstrates two quick tricks to get more flavor from a fast entree: Cook the herbs or spices first in butter or oil to develop flavor; then roll the chicken in the flavored butter before cooking. For the four servings I use only a tablespoon each of butter and olive oil; most of the butter mixes with the cooking juices and can be discarded before serving if you need to cut back on fats. You may be surprised about how much flavor you can get as well from the microwave oven version.

Preparation time: 5 minutes
Cooking time: 10 minutes
Serves: 2–4

1 tablespoon butter
1 tablespoon olive oil
½ teaspoon fennel seeds
4 chicken thighs, skinned and boned
¼ teaspoon salt
⅛ teaspoon freshly ground black pepper

1. Melt butter and oil over medium heat in a large, nonstick skillet. Add fennel seeds; cook and stir 1–2 minutes, until seeds soften slightly and give off an aroma.
2. Add chicken in single layer. Cook over medium heat 4–6 minutes, turning once, until golden on both sides. Cover pan tightly. Cook 4–6 minutes, until juices run clear. Sprinkle with salt and pepper. Spoon juices over chicken just before serving.

MICROWAVE OVEN METHOD—5 minutes: (1) Reduce the butter and olive oil by half, and put on a dinner-size plate. Do not cover. MICROWAVE (high) 1–2 minutes to melt butter. Stir in fennel seeds. Do not cover. MICROWAVE (high) 1–2 minutes, until seeds soften slightly and give off an aroma. (2) Turn the chicken thighs several times in the flavored butter. Arrange chicken on the plate with the thickest portions to the outside. Cover with plastic wrap, vented. MICROWAVE (high) 3–4 minutes, until chicken is no longer pink in the center and the juices run clear, turning chicken over after 2 minutes. Let stand 2 minutes. Sprinkle with salt and pepper. Spoon juices over chicken just before serving.

TIP: *If thighs are not boned, they will need another 1–2 minutes to cook. For cooking times for other chicken parts, check the Microwave Chicken Cooking Chart (see Index).*

LEMON-CHIVE CHICKEN

This basic recipe can be used with a variety of herbs—such as tarragon, dill, basil, rosemary, thyme, oregano, or parsley—for a different dish each time. The herbs add not just flavor but a touch of color to the pale chicken.

I am generous with mild-tasting chives in this dish. If you are using other, stronger-tasting fresh herbs, start with just 1 tablespoon; if using dried herbs, you'll need only ½ teaspoon.

Preparation time: 2 minutes
Cooking time: 8 minutes
Serves: 4

2 whole chicken breasts (4 halves), skinned and boned
¼ cup Basic Chicken Stock (see Index) or chicken broth
1 tablespoon lemon juice
2 tablespoons chopped fresh chives
¼ teaspoon salt
⅛ teaspoon freshly ground black pepper

1. Place chicken breasts between two sheets of waxed paper and lightly pound to ¼-inch thick. Put chicken in a single layer in a large, nonstick skillet. Add Basic Chicken Stock and lemon juice. Heat to simmer. Cover and simmer over medium heat 6 minutes, until center of chicken is no longer pink.
2. Remove chicken to a serving platter; keep warm. Gently boil pan juices 1–2 minutes, until reduced by half. Stir in chives, salt, and pepper; spoon over chicken.

MICROWAVE OVEN METHOD—4 minutes: Place chicken breasts between two sheets of waxed paper and lightly pound to ⅛-inch thick. Put chicken breasts on a plate with thickest portions to the outside. Eliminate Basic Chicken Stock. Drizzle with lemon juice. Cover with plastic wrap, vented. MICROWAVE (high) 4–6 minutes, until center of chicken is no longer pink. Stir in chives, salt, and pepper; spoon over chicken.

TIP: Check the Microwave Chicken Cooking Chart (see Index) for the cooking times of thighs and other chicken parts.

CHICKEN WITH SKINNY ASPARAGUS

Slender, spring asparagus cook in the microwave with no extra effort on the same plate as the chicken for dinner. (Big, thick asparagus—which I prefer for flavor—will need to be cut into diagonal slices to cook in the same amount of time.)

Preparation time: 5 minutes
Microwave time: 5 minutes
Serves: 4

2 **whole chicken breasts (4 halves), skinned and boned**
2 **tablespoons lemon juice**
½ **pound thin asparagus, ends trimmed if necessary**
1 **tablespoon chopped fresh thyme** *or* ½ **teaspoon dried**
¼ **teaspoon salt**
⅛ **teaspoon freshly ground black pepper**
4 **lemon wedges**

Arrange chicken on a rim of a large plate, with thickest portions to the outside. Drizzle with lemon juice. Arrange asparagus in the center. Cover with plastic wrap, vented. MICROWAVE (high) 5–7 minutes, until chicken is no longer pink in the center, turning chicken over and rearranging asparagus once. Drain. Sprinkle chicken with thyme, salt, and pepper. Serve with lemon wedges.

TIP: To help the asparagus cook evenly, arrange the tips toward the center and the ends of the stalks toward the outside of the plate where they will cook faster.

TIP: If you have a little more time to cook, try Sesame Chicken and Asparagus (see Index).

CHERVIL CHUNKS

A quick dish for two people: Chicken chunks are rolled in melted butter, cooked, then sprinkled with fresh chervil. Easy, fast.

Preparation time: 5 minutes
Cooking time: 6 minutes
Serves: 2

1 tablespoon butter or
   margarine
1 whole chicken breast
   (2 halves), skinned, boned,
   and cut into 1-inch chunks
1 tablespoon chopped fresh
   chervil *or* ½ teaspoon dried
¼ teaspoon salt
⅛ teaspoon freshly ground black
   pepper

Melt butter over medium heat in a medium, nonstick skillet. Toss chicken in butter to coat. Cook and stir 5–6 minutes, until chicken is golden on the outside and center is no longer pink. Stir in chervil, salt, and pepper.

MICROWAVE OVEN METHOD—(1) Put butter or margarine on a dinner or pie plate. MICROWAVE (high) 30 seconds to 1 minute to melt. (2) Toss chicken in butter to coat. Push chicken to rim of plate, leaving a little room between pieces. Cover with plastic wrap, vented. MICROWAVE (high) 3–4 minutes, until centers of chicken pieces are no longer pink, stirring once. Toss chicken in cooking juices, then drain or remove to serving dish. Sprinkle with chervil, salt, and pepper.

BUTTERCRUMB CHICKEN

Cooked in the microwave, chicken breasts topped with buttery bread crumbs make a fast dinner treat.

Preparation time: 5 minutes
Microwave time: 7 minutes
Serves: 4

**2 whole chicken breasts
  (4 halves), skinned and boned
8 tablespoons (1 stick) butter
½ cup fine dry bread crumbs
1 teaspoon lemon juice
4 lemon wedges**

1. Arrange chicken on a plate with thickest portions to the outside. Cover with plastic wrap, vented. MICROWAVE (high) 4–6 minutes, until center of chicken is no longer pink, turning chicken pieces over after 3 minutes. Let stand 2 minutes on the counter. Drain.
2. Put butter in a 4-cup measure. MICROWAVE (high) 2–3 minutes, until butter is hot and frothy. Stir in crumbs. MICROWAVE (high) 1–2 minutes, until bubbly. Stir in lemon juice. Arrange chicken on serving plates and spoon buttery crumbs on top. Garnish with lemon wedges.

TIP: To cut back on cholesterol, substitute margarine for butter. You may also use half the amount of butter or margarine and bread crumbs; if you do, squeeze some extra lemon juice over the chicken before adding the topping.

ONE-PLATE CHICKEN AND VEGETABLES

This one-plate entree is one of the best examples of fine and fast microwave cooking. In about 2 more minutes than it takes to cook four chicken breasts, an assortment of fresh vegetables cook to al dente right on the same plate. I like to use this recipe at the end of the week when there is a little of this and that left in the refrigerator. Chicken—with a little mushrooms, a lone zucchini, a handful of spinach, and a sweet carrot—makes the start of a fine meal.

Preparation time: 10 minutes
Microwave time: 6 minutes
Serves: 4

2 whole chicken breasts (4 halves), skinned and boned
2 cups of one or more vegetables (see Tip)
¼ teaspoon salt
⅛ teaspoon freshly ground black pepper
2 tablespoons minced fresh parsley

Arrange chicken around rim of a large plate, thickest portions to the outside. Place fast-cooking vegetables in the center, slow-cooking vegetables close to or even between chicken breasts. Cover with plastic wrap, vented. MICROWAVE (high) 6–8 minutes, until center of chicken is no longer pink and vegetables are tender, turning chicken pieces over once. Drain. Sprinkle with salt, pepper, and parsley.

TIP: Dense or large vegetables take more time to cook in the microwave oven than light-textured, cut-up vegetables. For best results, place fast-cooking vegetables in the center of the plate, and slow-cooking vegetables toward the rim. Because the chicken takes up so much room around the plate, you'll have the most success if you use primarily fast-cooking vegetables.

Fast-cooking vegetables: asparagus tips, broccoli tips, thinly sliced green cabbage, rinsed frozen corn, sliced fennel, peeled garlic, sliced jicama, julienned leeks, sliced mushrooms, sliced onions, rinsed frozen peas, sliced sweet peppers, radishes, snow peas, spinach, sliced summer squash, tomato wedges, sliced zucchini.

Slow-cooking vegetables: sliced broccoli stems, brussels sprouts, julienned carrots, green beans, julienned celery, sliced Kohlrabi, julienned parsnips, fresh peas, sliced potatoes, sliced red cabbage, sliced rutabagas, sliced winter squash, sliced sweet potatoes, sliced turnips.

TIP: Need to cook even more vegetables? Pile up to 6 cups of cut-up vegetables in a large bowl, placing the fast-cooking vegetables in the center, and the slow-cooking vegetables around the rim. Cover with plastic wrap, vented. MICROWAVE (high) 4–5 minutes, or until the vegetables are tender. Let stand 2 minutes to finish cooking. Drain. Add salt, pepper, and chopped fresh parsley.

CASSEROLES

Chicken blends beautifully into casserole dishes with vegetables, herbs, pasta, and rice. And these multi-item dishes can be ready fairly fast.

Almond Chicken and Rice, in which juices from the chicken are absorbed into the rice for extra flavor, is ready in less than 25 minutes. Family-style Chicken-Stuffed Peppers, updated with chicken instead of ground beef, can be cooked in a conventional oven or, if you are short on time, in just 20 minutes in the microwave oven.

I've broadened the definition of casserole to include dishes such as Chicken Vesuvio, in which chicken, potatoes, olive oil, and wine bake together until flavors meld. Look to this chapter, too, for dishes that are ideal for bring-a-dish parties: Green Rice and Chicken, Shrimp-Chicken-Bean Chop, and Indian-Spiced Rice with Chicken.

ALMOND CHICKEN AND RICE

You'll become addicted to this super-efficient dish, which can be started a minute after you walk in the house and finished less than 20 minutes later. The chicken cooks right along with the rice (the juices from the chicken are absorbed by the rice), and all you need to do for supper is add a vegetable or salad.

Preparation time: 10 minutes
Cooking time: 15 minutes
Serves: 4

1¼ cups uncooked long-grain rice
  3 cups Basic Chicken Stock (see Index) or chicken broth
  ½ teaspoon salt
  ¼ teaspoon almond extract
  2 tablespoons lemon juice
  1 whole chicken breast (2 halves), skinned, boned, and cubed
  ⅓ cup finely sliced almonds, toasted
  2 tablespoons chopped fresh chives

1. Put rice, Basic Chicken Stock, salt, almond extract, and lemon juice in a 2½-quart saucepan. Cover. Heat to boil. Reduce heat; simmer 10 minutes.
2. Add chicken. Simmer 5–7 minutes, until the rice is tender and the chicken pieces are no longer pink in the center. Stir in almonds and chives.

MICROWAVE OVEN METHOD—19 minutes: (1) Put rice, only 1¾ cups Basic Chicken Stock, salt, almond extract, and lemon juice in a 2½-quart casserole. Cover. MICROWAVE (high) 5–7 minutes to boiling, then MICROWAVE (medium) 5–7 minutes, until rice is partially cooked. (2) Stir in almonds and chicken. MICROWAVE (medium) 9–11 minutes, until chicken is no longer pink and liquid is absorbed. Stir in almonds and chives.

CHICKEN VESUVIO

Chicken Vesuvio is a popular specialty in Chicago's Italian restaurants. For this lighter version, I've included the most important taste elements—garlic, olive oil, and oregano—but reduced the total oil. I prefer the dark meat of drumsticks in this dish, but you may substitute all white meat or a cut-up fryer.

Preparation time: 10 minutes
Cooking time: 1 hour
Serves: 4

  8 chicken drumsticks
1½ pounds unpeeled baking
     potatoes, washed and cut
     into lengthwise wedges
  1 tablespoon minced fresh
     oregano *or* 1 teaspoon dried
 ½ teaspoon dried sage
 ½ teaspoon salt
 ¼ teaspoon freshly ground
     black pepper
 ¼ cup olive oil
  2 tablespoons minced garlic
 ¼ cup dry white wine or
     vermouth
  2 tablespoons minced fresh
     parsley

1. Heat oven to 375°F. Put chicken and potatoes in a 13" × 9" nonstick baking pan. Sprinkle with oregano, sage, salt, and pepper. Drizzle with oil. Bake 30 minutes, stirring once to turn pieces over.
2. Sprinkle with garlic and wine. Continue baking 30 minutes, until chicken juices run clear and potatoes are tender. Drizzle pan juices over chicken and potatoes on a platter, sprinkle with parsley, and serve.

TIP: *To further reduce fats, skin the chicken before cooking. After you have pulled the skin halfway off a drumstick, grab the slippery skin with a paper towel and yank the rest off.*

CHICKEN-STUFFED PEPPERS

I've updated a favorite family-style dish here, replacing ground beef with chicken. The herbs and cheese are kept simple to appeal to children.

Preparation time: 25 minutes
Cooking time: 1 hour
Serves: 4

4 medium to large sweet green bell peppers
2 tablespoons oil
½ cup chopped onion
1 teaspoon minced garlic
2 whole chicken breasts (4 halves), skinned, boned, and cut into ½-inch cubes
1 cup cooked rice
½ teaspoon salt
¼ teaspoon freshly ground black pepper
2 tablespoons chopped fresh basil *or* 2 teaspoons dried
2 teaspoons chopped fresh oregano *or* ½ teaspoon dried
2 cups Fresh Tomato Sauce (see Index) *or* 1 15-ounce can tomato sauce
1 cup shredded cheddar

1. Slice off stem ends of green peppers. Remove seeds and white membranes. Rinse.
2. Cook peppers in a large pot of boiling water 5 minutes, until crisp-tender. Remove and rinse under cold water to stop cooking.
3. Heat oven to 350°F. Heat oil in a large skillet; add onion and garlic. Cook and stir 2 minutes. Stir in chicken; cook 4 minutes, until centers of chicken pieces are no longer pink. Stir in rice, salt, pepper, basil, and oregano.
4. Stuff peppers with chicken mixture. Place in a 2-quart casserole. Pour Fresh Tomato Sauce over the peppers. Bake uncovered 40 minutes. Sprinkle with cheese. Bake 10 minutes, until the cheese melts.

MICROWAVE OVEN METHOD—17 minutes: (1) Follow Step 1. (2) Eliminate oil. Put chicken, onion, and garlic in a 2-quart rectangular casserole. MICROWAVE (high) 4–5 minutes, until chicken is no longer pink, stirring twice. Drain. Mix in rice, salt, pepper, basil, and oregano. (3) Stuff peppers with chicken mixture. Place in casserole, separating peppers as much as possible. Pour Fresh Tomato Sauce over peppers. (4) Cover with waxed paper. MICROWAVE (high) 3 minutes. MICROWAVE (medium) 10–12 minutes, until just tender. Let stand, covered, 2 minutes. Sprinkle with cheese. (The heat from the peppers will melt the cheese.) Spoon extra sauce from the pan over the peppers as you serve them.

TIP: For extra goodness, you may opt not to drain the chicken juices in Step 2. The peppers will ooze with juices—tasty but messy.

GREEN RICE AND CHICKEN

The green color in this rice dish comes from a healthy assortment of spinach, parsley, and chives.

Preparation time: 10 minutes
Cooking time: 25 minutes
Serves: 4

2 tablespoons butter or margarine
2 tablespoons minced onion
1 cup uncooked rice
2¾ cups Basic Chicken Stock (see Index) or chicken broth
1 whole chicken breast (2 halves), skinned, boned, and cubed
1 10-ounce package frozen chopped spinach, defrosted and well drained
¼ cup chopped fresh parsley
½ teaspoon salt
⅛ teaspoon freshly ground black pepper
1 tablespoon chopped fresh chives
¼ cup sour cream or grated Romano cheese (optional)

1. Melt butter in a 2½-quart saucepan. Stir in onion; cook and stir 2 minutes, to soften. Stir in rice and Basic Chicken Stock. Heat to boil; simmer, covered, 10 minutes.
2. Stir in chicken. Simmer, covered, 5 minutes. Stir in spinach, parsley, salt, and pepper. Simmer, covered, 5 minutes. Fluff with fork. Stir in chives and sour cream or cheese.

MICROWAVE OVEN METHOD—22 minutes: (1) Put butter or margarine and onion in a 2½-quart casserole. MICROWAVE (high) 2–3 minutes to soften. Stir in rice and Basic Chicken Stock. Cover. MICROWAVE (high) 5–7 minutes, until boiling. MICROWAVE (medium) 10–12 minutes, until rice is almost tender but still moist. (2) Arrange chicken pieces on top of the rice, around the edge of the casserole. Cover. MICROWAVE (high) 3–5 minutes, until centers of chicken pieces are no longer pink, stirring and separating chicken pieces once. (3) Stir in spinach, parsley, salt, and pepper. MICROWAVE (high) 2–3 minutes to warm through. Fluff with fork. Stir in chives and, if desired, sour cream or Romano.

TIP: In microwave cooking, you don't need fats to keep the food from sticking, so you may wish to eliminate both the butter or margarine and the optional sour cream or Romano cheese when following the microwave oven cooking directions.

FENNEL CHICKEN AU GRATIN

Fennel's unusual, sweet licorice or anise flavor mellows as it cooks and adds a distinctive flavor to this casserole. The buttered bread-crumb topping gets 3 minutes under the broiler to brown and crisp.

Preparation time: 15 minutes
Cooking time: 15 minutes
Serves: 4–6

2 fennel bulbs
4 tablespoons (½ stick) butter
1 whole chicken breast (2 halves), skinned, boned, and cubed
2 medium tomatoes, diced
¼ teaspoon salt
⅛ teaspoon freshly ground black pepper
1 teaspoon fresh lemon juice
2 tablespoons minced fresh parsley
⅛ teaspoon cayenne
½ cup fresh bread crumbs

1. Trim thin stalks from the fennel bulbs, reserving some of the edible, feathery leaves for garnish. Cut bulbs in half. Discard outer layers if woody. Leave cores to hold layers intact. Cut bulbs into thin slices.
2. Cook fennel in boiling water 3 minutes, until crisp-tender. Drain and rinse under cold water to stop cooking.
3. Heat broiler to high. Melt 1 tablespoon butter in a large skillet. Add chicken; cook and stir 5 minutes until no longer pink. Stir in tomatoes, fennel, salt, and pepper.
4. Put chicken mixture in an 8-inch square baking dish. Put remaining 3 tablespoons butter in the same skillet from Step 3. Heat over low heat until melted. Stir in lemon juice, parsley, and cayenne. Stir in bread crumbs.
5. Sprinkle bread crumbs over chicken. Broil 2–3 minutes, until crumbs are lightly browned. Sprinkle with a few of the reserved fennel leaves.

TIP: Fennel, also called Florentine fennel, sweet fennel, or finocchio, is related to celery, carrots, and parsley. Its foliage is edible and makes a fine garnish, but the vegetable is prized mostly for its white bulb, which grows aboveground. Fennel seeds come from a related herb.

Look for fennel from early fall to early spring. Save some choice slices to serve raw with Parmesan or chèvre and a sweet, red dessert wine.

CORN MAQUE CHICKEN

Maque choux, literally "false cabbage" in French, is an old Louisiana dish with numerous variations. Originally it was made with a type of Indian corn, eaten cob and all, that tasted somewhat like cabbage. The dish no longer tastes like cabbage, but the name stuck. In this version, we throw in some chicken as a hearty lagniappe.

Preparation time: 10 minutes
Cooking time: 15 minutes
Serves: 4

2 tablespoons vegetable oil
2 tablespoons butter
½ cup minced onion
3 or 4 chicken thighs, skinned, boned, and cut into 1-inch cubes
4 cups fresh or frozen corn kernels
2 tablespoons sugar
¼ teaspoon salt
½ teaspoon freshly ground white pepper
¼ teaspoon cayenne
½ cup evaporated milk
1 egg
Chopped fresh chives or parsley

1. Heat oil and butter in a 10-inch, nonstick skillet. Add onion; cook and stir 2 minutes. Stir in chicken, corn, sugar, salt, pepper, and cayenne. Cook, covered, over medium-low heat 10 minutes.

2. Uncover. Cook at a medium boil until liquid thickens. Add half the evaporated milk (¼ cup); boil 3 minutes.

3. In a small bowl, whisk remaining milk and the egg until frothy. Stir into corn. Serve hot, sprinkled with chives or parsley.

LINGUINE WITH CALIFORNIA SAUCE

Sweet, sun-dried tomatoes add a fillip to this chicken-enhanced pasta dish. The pasta itself is best made conventionally on the stove, but you can make the sauce either on the stove or in the microwave oven.

Preparation time: 10 minutes
Cooking time: 15 minutes
Serves: 6

1 **medium leek**
1 **tablespoon butter**
3 **tablespoons olive oil**
1 **tablespoon minced garlic**
2 **14-ounce cans plum tomatoes, chopped coarse, ¼ cup juices reserved**
2 **whole chicken breasts (4 halves), skinned, boned, and cubed**
2 **teaspoons finely chopped fresh oregano** *or* **½ teaspoon dried**
¼ **teaspoon salt**
⅛ **teaspoon freshly ground black pepper**
3 **ounces (1 cup) dry-pack sun-dried tomatoes,** *or* **½ cup oil-pack, chopped coarse (see Tip)**
1 **pound linguine, cooked, drained**
2 **tablespoons chopped fresh parsley**
2 **tablespoons chopped fresh basil**

1. Cut off root end of leek. Trim away all but 2 inches of green. Slice in half lengthwise and wash well under running water, separating stalk sections to remove dirt. Chop.
2. Heat butter and 2 tablespoons of the oil in a large saucepan. Add leek and garlic; cook and stir 3 minutes, until softened.
3. Stir in plum tomatoes, chicken, oregano, salt, and pepper. Cover. Simmer, stirring often, 10 minutes, until center of chicken is no longer pink.
4. Stir in sun-dried tomatoes. Cover. Simmer 5 minutes to heat through. Toss linguine with remaining tablespoon olive oil. Serve topped with tomato sauce. Sprinkle with parsley and basil.

MICROWAVE OVEN METHOD—*12 minutes: (1) Follow Step 1. (2) Put butter, 2 tablespoons of the olive oil, leek, and garlic in a 2-quart casserole. MICROWAVE (high) 2–3 minutes to soften. Stir in plum tomatoes, chicken, oregano, salt, and pepper. Cover. MICROWAVE (high)*

8–10 minutes, until center of chicken is no longer pink, stirring twice. (3) Stir in sun-dried tomatoes. Cover. MICROWAVE (high) 2–3 minutes to heat through. Toss linguine with remaining tablespoon olive oil. Serve topped with tomato sauce. Sprinkle with parsley and basil.

TIP: *If sun-dried tomatoes are packed in oil, you can use this oil in Step 2 (conventional and microwave oven method directions). If sun-dried tomatoes are not packed in oil, cover them with water and MICROWAVE (high) 1–2 minutes, until almost boiling. Let stand for a half hour to soften.*

If dried tomatoes still feel tough, process in a food processor with some of the cooked tomato sauce, then return to casserole.

SHRIMP-CHICKEN-BEAN CHOP

Shrimp, chicken, and fresh green beans are chopped and mixed with pungent fresh ginger and aromatic sesame oil for a dish with an Oriental twist. Serve over brown rice.

Preparation time: 15 minutes
Cooking time: 15 minutes
Serves: 6–8

1 **pound green beans, ends trimmed, chopped into ¼-inch pieces**
1 **tablespoon vegetable oil**
1 **whole chicken breast (2 halves), skinned, boned, and cut into ½-inch pieces**
1 **cup raw fresh or defrosted shrimp, shelled, cleaned, and chopped coarse**
1 **teaspoon minced fresh ginger**
1 **teaspoon minced garlic**
2 **tablespoons soy sauce**
1 **teaspoon sesame oil**
Salt to taste
2 **tablespoons cornstarch, dissolved in 2 tablespoons water**
¼ **cup chopped fresh coriander (cilantro)**

1. Cook green beans in boiling water 6–7 minutes, until crisp-tender. Drain. Reserve.
2. Heat wok or a large skillet over medium-high heat until hot. Add vegetable oil; heat until hot but not smoking. Add chicken; stir-fry 4 minutes, until chicken is no longer pink. Add beans; stir-fry 1 minute.
3. Stir in shrimp; cook and stir 2 minutes, until just opaque. Stir in ginger, garlic, soy sauce, sesame oil, salt, and cornstarch mixture. Cook and stir 1 minute, until thickened. Serve immediately sprinkled generously with coriander.

TIP: *The cooking time for the beans will depend on their freshness and size. Smaller, fresh beans—with a higher water content—will cook faster.*

INDIAN-SPICED RICE WITH CHICKEN

For this hearty casserole (featured on the book cover), a whole, cut-up chicken is browned, then added to rice and spices. The chicken picks up the flavors from the spices, and the rice benefits from both the spices and the natural chicken juices. For a similar dish with less meat, try the Microwaved Indian-Spiced Rice with Chicken (see Index).

Preparation time: 15 minutes
Cooking time: 1 hour
Serves: 4

2 tablespoons olive oil
1 whole chicken, cut up into 6-8 pieces, breasts and legs skinned
½ cup chopped onion
1 teaspoon minced garlic
¼ teaspoon ground cumin
½ teaspoon ground coriander
¼ teaspoon ground turmeric
⅛ teaspoon (scant) ground cinnamon
½ teaspoon salt
¼ teaspoon freshly ground black pepper
¼ cup raisins (1 ½-ounce box), preferably golden yellow
1¼ cups uncooked rice
2½ cups Basic Chicken Stock (see Index) or chicken broth
¼ cup frozen peas, thawed
¼ cup finely sliced almonds
2 green onions, white portion and first 2 inches of green, chopped

1. Heat oven to 350°F. Heat oil in a large, nonstick skillet. Brown chicken on all sides, 10 minutes. Remove. Stir in onion and garlic; cook and stir 2 minutes, until soft. Remove from heat; stir in cumin, coriander, turmeric, cinnamon, salt, pepper, and raisins.
2. Put rice, Basic Chicken Stock, and onion mixture into a 3-quart shallow casserole dish. Mix well. Add chicken. Cover with foil.
3. Bake 40 minutes. Uncover; continue baking 10–15 minutes, until liquid is absorbed and juices from the chicken run clear. Sprinkle with peas and almonds. Let stand, covered, 5 minutes. Top with green onions.

TIP: Turmeric, a natural dye, will temporarily stain your counter a lovely yellow if you carelessly set down your mixing spoon.

MICROWAVED INDIAN-SPICED RICE WITH CHICKEN

This lighter version of Indian-Spiced Rice uses boneless chicken breasts instead of a whole, cut-up chicken. It's a little faster to cook, and the technique for cooking rice is foolproof. For a dish that tastes so special, this is really quite easy to make.

Preparation time: 15 minutes
Microwave time: 22 minutes
Serves: 4

½ cup chopped onion
1 teaspoon minced garlic
½ teaspoon ground cumin
½ teaspoon ground coriander
¼ teaspoon ground turmeric
⅛ teaspoon (scant) ground cinnamon
½ teaspoon salt
¼ teaspoon freshly ground black pepper
1 tablespoon olive oil
1¼ cups uncooked rice
1¾ cups Basic Chicken Stock (see Index) or chicken broth
1 whole chicken breast (2 halves), skinned, boned, and cubed
¼ cup raisins (1 ½-ounce box), preferably golden yellow
¼ cup finely sliced almonds
¼ cup frozen peas
2 green onions, white portion and first 2 inches of green, chopped

1. Mix onion, garlic, cumin, coriander, turmeric, cinnamon, salt, pepper, and olive oil in a 2½-quart casserole. Do not cover. MICROWAVE (high) 3–4 minutes, until onion is quite tender.
2. Add rice and Basic Chicken Stock. Cover. MICROWAVE (high) 5–7 minutes to boiling, then MICROWAVE (medium) 5–7 minutes, until rice is partially cooked.
3. Stir in chicken, raisins, and almonds. MICROWAVE (medium) 9–11 minutes, until chicken is no longer pink and liquid is absorbed. Rinse peas under cold water to defrost. Stir into rice. Let stand, covered, 3 minutes. Top with green onions.

LIGHT FARE

The trick to eating light is to add enough taste items to the plain chicken to keep the taste interesting.

Eggplant and Chicken with Oyster Sauce does the trick. So does the wonderful Ginger-Garlic Thighs. A little wine and herbs substitute for butter in Chicken with Wine and Herbs. This kind of cooking is light cooking at its best.

You'll find a wealth of other light dishes throughout this book. In most cases you can substitute lighter chicken breasts for thighs or legs and save even more fat and calories.

GINGER-GARLIC THIGHS

Fresh garlic and ginger contribute a lot of flavor, and the soy sauce adds a light brown color to this simple dish. A little cornstarch is added to thicken the flavored cooking juices.

Preparation time: 5 minutes
Cooking time: 45 minutes
Serves: 2–4

4 chicken thighs, skinned
2 teaspoons minced fresh ginger
2 teaspoons minced fresh garlic
2 tablespoons soy sauce
¼ teaspoon sesame oil
¼ cup Basic Chicken Stock (see Index) or chicken broth
2 teaspoons cornstarch dissolved in 2 tablespoons water
Chopped green onions

1. Heat oven to 350°F. Put chicken in a nonstick baking pan.
2. Mix ginger, garlic, soy sauce, sesame oil, and Basic Chicken Stock in a small bowl. Pour over chicken; turn to coat with soy mixture.
3. Bake, 40–45 minutes, turning chicken occasionally to coat with juices, until chicken is no longer pink near the bone. Remove chicken to a plate. Put pan over medium heat; add cornstarch mixture; cook and stir 2 minutes to thicken, then pour over chicken. Serve sprinkled with green onions.

MICROWAVE OVEN METHOD—8 minutes: (1) Because the quick cooking better retains the potency of garlic and ginger, reduce to 1 teaspoon each. Put ginger, garlic, soy sauce, and sesame oil (eliminate the Basic Chicken Stock) in a 1-cup measure. MICROWAVE (high), uncovered, 30 seconds to 1 minute to soften. (2) Arrange thighs on a plate with thickest portions to the outside. Pour ginger mixture over chicken and turn pieces to coat. Cover with plastic wrap, vented. MICROWAVE (high) 6–8 minutes, until chicken meat is no longer pink, turning pieces over once. Let stand 2 minutes. (3) Pour juices into a 1-cup measure. Spoon off excess fat and discard. Stir in dissolved cornstarch. MICROWAVE (high), uncovered, 1–2 minutes to thicken. Pour thickened juices over chicken, sprinkle with green onions, and serve.

TIP: For more flavor, marinate chicken in soy mixture 30 minutes to 1 hour before baking.

TIP: If you use chicken breasts (bone in), cooking time will be 30–35 minutes.

TWO-PEPPER CHICKEN

Eye appeal—provided by overlapping strips of green and yellow, orange and yellow, or even red and black sweet peppers—makes this microwave dish look more complicated than it is. In fact, it is very easy: The chicken and colorful peppers cook simultaneously on the same plate. No fuss. No fat.

Preparation time: 15 minutes
Microwave time: 5 minutes
Serves: 4

2 sweet bell peppers of different colors (see Tip)
2 whole chicken breasts (4 halves), skinned and boned
2 tablespoons fresh basil *or* 1 teaspoon dried
¼ teaspoon salt
⅛ teaspoon freshly ground black pepper

1. Slice off tops of peppers and save for another use. Remove cores and white membranes. Cut into julienne strips.
2. Arrange chicken along rim of a plate, with thickest portions to the outside. Layer pepper strips in the center. Cover with plastic wrap, vented. MICROWAVE (high) 5–7 minutes, until center of chicken is no longer pink and vegetables are tender-crisp. Drain.
3. Arrange chicken on bed of peppers, with a few peppers on top for garnish. Sprinkle with basil, salt, and pepper.

TIP: *The beautiful tulip-yellow and extraordinary black—actually deep purple—peppers on grocery shelves hail from Holland, which helps explain the high price tags attached to these novelties. The flavors are a bit milder and sweeter than those of green varieties.*

Although yellow and orange peppers hold their colors well, black ones tend to fade to green when cooked. If you want the look of the black peppers, add them raw just before serving.

CHICKEN WITH PEA PODS

Only a scant tablespoon of oil is needed to cook this colorful, healthful dish of chicken and crisp pea pods. Serve with rice.

Preparation time: 15 minutes
Cooking time: 6 minutes
Serves: 2–4

2 tablespoons soy sauce
2 tablespoons dry white wine or vermouth
¼ teaspoon sesame oil
¼ teaspoon freshly ground black pepper
1 teaspoon cornstarch, dissolved in 1 tablespoon water
1 tablespoon vegetable oil
2 teaspoons minced fresh garlic
2 teaspoons minced fresh ginger
1 whole chicken breast (2 halves), skinned, boned, and cut into ½-inch-wide strips
¼ pound snow peas, ends trimmed, top and bottom threads removed
1 8-ounce can baby corn cobs
2 green onions, white portion and first 2 inches of green, sliced

1. Mix soy sauce, wine, sesame oil, pepper, and cornstarch mixture in a small bowl. Set aside.
2. Heat wok or a large skillet over medium heat until hot. Add vegetable oil. Heat until hot. Add garlic and ginger; stir-fry 20 seconds. Add chicken; stir-fry 3 minutes, until no longer pink. Add snow peas; stir-fry 1 minute. Add corn; stir-fry 30 seconds. Add soy sauce mixture; stir-fry until thickened. Sprinkle with green onions and serve immediately.

TIP: A small can of rinsed and drained bamboo shoots may be substituted for the corn cobs.

CHICKEN WITH WINE AND HERBS

Light doesn't have to mean dull. These lean chicken breasts are drizzled with a little wine and fresh herbs, then quickly cooked. I like to cover the chicken in the microwave method loosely with waxed paper to allow the alcohol from the wine to evaporate.

Preparation time: 5 minutes
Microwave time: 6 minutes
Serves: 4

**2 whole chicken breasts
   (4 halves), skinned and boned
2 tablespoons dry white wine
2 tablespoons water
2 teaspoons fresh tarragon** *or*
   **½ teaspoon dried
¼ teaspoon salt
⅛ teaspoon freshly ground black
   pepper**

Place chicken between sheets of waxed paper and pound to ¼-inch thick. Put all ingredients into a large, nonstick skillet. Heat to simmer. Cover tightly; simmer over medium-low heat 6–8 minutes, until juices run clear. Remove cover. Remove chicken to a plate. Boil juices gently 2 minutes, until some of the juices evaporate. Pour over chicken.

MICROWAVE OVEN METHOD—6 minutes: Place chicken between sheets of waxed paper and pound to ¼-inch thick. Put the chicken on a plate with thickest portions to the outside. Drizzle with wine. (Eliminate the 2 tablespoons water.) Sprinkle with herbs, salt, and pepper. Cover loosely with waxed paper. MICROWAVE (high) 6–8 minutes, until center of chicken is no longer pink, turning chicken over after 3–4 minutes. Let stand, covered, 2 minutes. Spoon juices over chicken just before serving.

SESAME CHICKEN AND ASPARAGUS

Chicken strips absorb a tasty Oriental marinade, then are quick-cooked and tossed with sliced, fresh asparagus. Serve with rice.

Preparation time: 15 minutes
Cooking time: 10 minutes
Serves: 4

2 **tablespoons vegetable oil**
1 **tablespoon soy sauce**
¼ **teaspoon sesame oil**
1 **teaspoon minced fresh ginger**
1 **tablespoon dry sherry**
2 **whole chicken breasts
   (4 halves), skinned, boned,
   and cut into ¾-inch strips**
½ **pound thin asparagus, cut
   into 2-inch diagonal slices**
2 **teaspoons sesame seeds**
2 **green onions, white portion
   and first 2 inches of green,
   sliced**

1. Mix 1 tablespoon vegetable oil, soy sauce, sesame oil, ginger, and sherry in a medium bowl. Toss chicken in mixture and let marinate 10 minutes.
2. Cook asparagus in a large saucepan of boiling water, 3 minutes, until crisp-tender. Drain.
3. Heat wok or a large skillet over medium-high heat until hot. Add remaining 1 tablespoon vegetable oil; heat until hot but not smoking. Add chicken mixture; stir-fry 6 minutes, until chicken is no longer pink. Add asparagus; stir-fry 30 seconds. Sprinkle with sesame seeds and green onions.

MICROWAVE OVEN METHOD—6 minutes: (1) Follow Step 1. (2) Put asparagus on a dinner plate. Cover with plastic wrap, vented. MICROWAVE (high) 1½–2 minutes, until almost tender. Remove cover. (3) (Omit 1 tablespoon oil.) Arrange chicken around edges of plate and pour marinade over. Do not cover. MICROWAVE (high) 3½–5 minutes, until centers of chicken pieces are no longer pink, turning and rearranging chicken twice. Toss asparagus and chicken together and MICROWAVE (high) about 30 seconds to heat through. Toss again. Sprinkle with sesame seeds and green onions.

TIP: For perfect texture, add asparagus tips 30 seconds after stem pieces; tips take slightly less time to cook. Note that tender asparagus get a head start under plastic wrap for moist, even cooking; chicken is cooked uncovered for a firm, stir-fry effect.

EGGPLANT AND CHICKEN WITH OYSTER SAUCE

This is a fine example of how beautifully chicken can be handled in the microwave oven—and without any added fat. Eggplant and chicken are cut in the same shape to double the meaty image. Oyster sauce and the chili paste with garlic come in bottles; you'll find them in the Oriental section of your grocery. Serve over rice.

Preparation time: 10 minutes
Microwave time: 9 minutes
Serves: 4

1 whole chicken breast (2 halves) boned and cut into ¾-inch cubes
¼ cup oyster sauce
1 teaspoon chopped ginger
1 teaspoon minced garlic
½–1 teaspoon chili paste with garlic (optional)
1 medium eggplant, peeled and cut into ¾-inch cubes
¼ cup water
½ teaspoon salt
¼ cup chopped fresh coriader (cilantro)

1. Mix chicken, oyster sauce, ginger, garlic, and chili paste (if desired) in a 2-quart casserole. Let marinate while you prepare the eggplant.
2. Sprinkle eggplant with salt; let drain on paper towel 20–30 minutes.
3. Stir eggplant, water, and salt in a 1-quart casserole. Cover. MICROWAVE (high) 3–5 minutes, stirring once, until just tender. Drain. Reserve.
4. In original casserole, MICROWAVE (high) the chicken 4–5 minutes, until the centers of the chicken pieces are no longer pink, stirring several times. Do not cover, or the chicken will cook more like a stew than a stir-fry. Stir eggplant into chicken and mix well. Sprinkle with coriander.

SPICY CHICKEN CHAYOTE

Chayote, a crisp-textured, mild-tasting gourd popular in Mexican cooking, works beautifully in this hot pepper–spiked dish. Serve the dish with rice, or use it to fill taco shells, topped with cheese and hot sauce.

Preparation time: 15 minutes
Cooking time: 15 minutes
Serves: 4–6

2 medium chayote, peeled, cored, and cut into ¼-inch cubes (about 2 cups)
2 tablespoons oil
1 whole chicken breast (2 halves), skinned, boned, and cubed
1 cup minced onion
1 teaspoon minced garlic
1 teaspoon seeded, minced hot pepper
2 cups seeded, coarsely chopped fresh tomato, or 1 15-ounce can, drained
1 tablespoon red-wine vinegar
2 dashes Worcestershire sauce
¼ teaspoon salt
½ teaspoon sugar
2 tablespoons chopped fresh coriander (cilantro)

1. Cook chayote in a large saucepan of boiling water, 5 minutes, until crisp-tender. Drain. Set aside.
2. Heat oil in a large, nonstick skillet over medium heat until hot. Add chicken, onion, garlic, and hot pepper. Sauté 5–6 minutes, or until chicken is no longer pink.
3. Stir in tomato, vinegar, Worcestershire sauce, salt, and sugar. Cook, uncovered, stirring often, over medium heat, 5 minutes, until juices reduce slightly. Stir in cooked chayote. Cook 1 minute. Sprinkle with coriander.

TIP: To prepare a fresh chayote, first cut off thin slices from both bumpy ends. Discard ends. Cut rest in half lengthwise. Peel as you would an apple.

Use a serrated tool (a grapefruit spoon works well) or melon baller to remove the white, pithy core and almond-shaped seed. Reserve edible seed. Discard core.

Turn chayote halves flat side down on cutting board. Cut into slices or cubes.

TIP: The chayote seed has an extraordinary taste, much like a fresh nut off a tree. If you're impatient, munch it raw. But the flavor deepens when the seed is cooked. Slip it into a dish for the last 2 minutes to cook.

MUSHROOM-STUFFED CHICKEN BREASTS

Chicken breasts are stuffed and rolled with a classic combination of fresh mushrooms, celery, and parsley, thickened with fresh bread crumbs, and enlivened with a touch of sherry.

Preparation time: 30 minutes
Cooking time: 30 minutes
Serves: 4

2 whole large chicken breasts (4 halves), skinned and boned
1 tablespoon butter or olive oil
½ cup thinly sliced celery
¼ cup minced fresh parsley
½ cup chopped fresh mushrooms
2 green onions, white portion and first 2 inches of green, chopped
½ cup fresh bread crumbs
2 tablespoons dry sherry or white wine
¼ teaspoon salt
⅛ teaspoon freshly ground black pepper
½ cup Basic Chicken Stock (see Index) or chicken broth

1. Remove all fat from chicken breasts and cut away any pieces of membrane. Rinse and pat dry. Place between two pieces of waxed paper and use a veal pounder or the side of a cleaver to pound each breast gently; flatten to about ⅛-inch thick. Set aside.

2. Heat oven to 350°F. Put butter or oil, celery, parsley, mushrooms, and green onions in a small, nonstick skillet. Cook and stir 3 minutes, until vegetables are soft. Stir in bread crumbs, sherry, salt, and pepper.

3. Spread mixture over four chicken breasts; roll chicken jelly-roll fashion and secure with toothpicks. Put chicken and Basic Chicken Stock into a lightly buttered or nonstick baking pan. Bake, covered, turning chicken occasionally, 20–25 minutes, until chicken turns from pink to white and is just firm to the touch. Cut each stuffed chicken breast into 1-inch slices and arrange attractively on serving dishes.

MICROWAVE OVEN METHOD—8 minutes: (1) Follow Step 1. (2) Eliminate butter or oil if desired. Put celery, parsley, mushrooms, and green onions in a 1-quart casserole. Cover. MICROWAVE (high) 3–4 minutes, until vegetables are soft. Stir in bread crumbs, sherry, salt, and pepper. (3) Spread mixture over four chicken breasts; roll chicken jelly-roll fashion and, if thick, secure with toothpicks. Arrange stuffed chicken breasts in a spokelike fashion on a dish or pie plate. (Eliminate the Basic Chicken Stock.) Cover with plastic wrap, vented. MICROWAVE (high) 5–7 minutes, until chicken turns from pink to white and is just firm to the touch, turning pieces after 3 minutes. Let stand 2 minutes. Cut each stuffed chicken breast into 1-inch slices and arrange attractively on serving dishes.

TIP: *The chicken breasts may be stuffed and stored, covered, in the refrigerator for several hours before cooking.*

REAL MEALS

Chicken has a reputation for being light—that is, low in calories and delicate in flavor. And the reputation is valid. But chicken can also be a real meal, hearty enough to satisfy big appetites.

Look in this chapter for recipes to satisfy the soul: Whole Roast Chicken with Buttermilk Gravy, Chicken-Eggplant Parmesan, or Whole Turkey with Apple-Walnut Dressing.

In many of the recipes, chicken is partnered with substantial vegetables—potatoes, broccoli, plantain, rutabagas—that fill without adding fat.

Real meals with chicken—the smart way to eat big.

MUSHROOM-SMOTHERED CHICKEN

A whole pound of beautiful, fresh mushrooms is cooked until soft and flavorful and generously piled over chicken breasts.

Preparation time: 15 minutes
Microwave time: 9 minutes
Serves: 4

2 whole chicken breasts, split (4 halves), skinned and boned
2 tablespoons butter
1 tablespoon olive oil
1 pound fresh mushrooms, wiped clean, sliced ¼-inch thick
1 small onion, sliced thin
1 tablespoon chopped fresh tarragon *or* ½ teaspoon dried
Salt and freshly ground black pepper to taste
2 tablespoons chopped fresh parsley

1. Place chicken breasts between pieces of waxed paper; use a veal pounder to pound breasts into ¼-inch-thick pieces. Set aside.
2. Heat butter and oil in a 12-inch, nonstick skillet. Sauté mushrooms, onion, and tarragon over medium-high heat for 5 minutes. Move to outside of skillet. Add chicken in a single layer. Brown both sides for about 3 minutes, total. Cover; cook 3 minutes. Uncover; cook about 2 minutes to evaporate juices. Add salt and pepper. Serve chicken smothered with mushrooms, sprinkled with parsley.

MICROWAVE OVEN METHOD—9 minutes: (1) Follow Step 1 above. (2) Put mushrooms, butter, and oil (cut butter and oil in half, if desired) in a 2-quart flat casserole. Cover. MICROWAVE (high) 3–4 minutes, until mushrooms start to soften. Stir in tarragon and chicken to moisten. Arrange chicken around edge of casserole, with thickest portions to the outside. Cover. MICROWAVE (high) 5–8 minutes, until center of chicken is no longer pink, turning over once. (3) Lift out chicken, set aside, and keep warm. Stir 2 tablespoons flour into mushrooms and juices. Do not cover. MICROWAVE (high) 1–2 minutes, until juices thicken. Add salt and pepper and serve as above.

TIP: This dish keeps well overnight, covered, in the refrigerator. Reheat, then spruce up with a sprinkling of freshly chopped tarragon, parsley, or green onion just before serving.

TIP: Vary this dish by adding different herbs such as basil, marjoram, or oregano.

CHICKEN-EGGPLANT PARMESAN

Slices of chicken and eggplant are layered, then covered with two cheeses and your favorite tomato sauce. The preparation is not very complicated; most of the time is needed to let the salted eggplant slices drain so that they won't be bitter. Serve with pasta.

Preparation time: 45 minutes
Cooking time: 40 minutes
Serves: 4

1 teaspoon salt
4 ½-inch slices peeled
   eggplant
¼ cup flour
1 egg
1 tablespoon water
½ cup fine bread crumbs
4–5 tablespoons olive oil
1 whole chicken breast
   (2 halves), skinned and
   boned
2 teaspoons chopped fresh
   oregano *or* ¼ teaspoon dried
1 cup shredded mozzarella
¼ cup grated Parmesan
2 cups tomato sauce (1
   15-ounce can)

1. Salt eggplant. Set in a colander and let drain 30 minutes; pat dry.
2. Heat oven to 325°F. Put flour on a plate. Crack egg into a small bowl; add water and lightly beat. Put bread crumbs on another plate. Dip eggplant slices in flour, then egg mixture, then in bread crumbs. Heat 2 tablespoons olive oil in a large, nonstick skillet. When hot, add eggplant; fry 3–4 minutes, until brown and crisp on both sides. Remove.
3. Pound chicken to about ⅛-inch thick between two pieces of waxed paper. Cut each breast half to make four somewhat square pieces. Dip in flour, then egg, then bread crumbs. Fry chicken, using more oil in the same pan, 4 minutes, until center of chicken is no longer pink, turning chicken once. Remove.
4. Arrange fried chicken and eggplant in a shallow, 2-quart baking dish. Sprinkle with oregano, three-fourths of the mozzarella, and half of the Parmesan. Spoon tomato sauce over all. Top with remaining cheeses. Bake, uncovered, 25 minutes, until sauce is bubbling hot.

TIP: *Avoid using carbon steel knives when cutting eggplant, as they leave grayish-black stains.*

CHICKEN-STUFFED POTATOES

Here's a whole meal—chicken, tomato, avocado, and cheese—stuffed into a baked potato. Add enough cheese to thicken the natural juices from the chicken and tomato, but keep the mixture juicy enough to moisten the potato without adding butter. If you love potatoes with a crisp skin, opt for the conventional oven method. Only have 15 minutes? You'll love the microwave option.

Preparation time: 20 minutes
Cooking time: 1 hour
Serves: 4

4 medium baking potatoes
2 tablespoons olive oil
2 teaspoons minced garlic
1 hot pepper, minced, with seeds
1 chicken breast (2 halves), skinned, boned, and cubed
1 ripe tomato, skinned and chopped rough
½ teaspoon salt
¼ teaspoon freshly ground black pepper
½ avocado, seeded, peeled, and cubed
1 tablespoon lemon juice
1½–2 cups grated cheddar
2 green onions, white portion and first 2 inches of green, sliced

1. Heat oven to 350°F. Scrub potatoes well. Bake, turning occasionally, 50–60 minutes, until fork tender.
2. Heat oil in a medium, nonstick skillet. Add garlic and hot pepper; cook and stir 1 minute. Add chicken; cook and stir 3–4 minutes, until chicken is no longer pink in the center. Stir in tomato; cook 2 minutes, until heated through. Add salt, pepper, avocado, lemon juice, and all but ¼ cup of cheese. Mix well.
3. Use a knife to split open potatoes; use a fork to fluff the insides of the potatoes. Spoon in chicken mixture and lightly mix. Sprinkle with remaining cheese and the green onion.

MICROWAVE OVEN METHOD—15 minutes: (1) Scrub potatoes well. Use a fork to prick potatoes several times. Place potatoes on a paper towel in the microwave oven. MICROWAVE (high) 10–12 minutes, until potatoes are just soft, turning towel 180 degrees after 6 minutes. Let stand on counter 3 minutes. (2) Put garlic, pepper, and 1 tablespoon olive oil (eliminate the other tablespoon of olive oil) in a 2-quart casserole. MICROWAVE (high) 1 minute to soften. Stir in chicken and tomato. Do not cover. MICROWAVE (high) 4–6 minutes, until chicken is no longer pink in the center, stirring twice (see Tip). Mix in salt, pepper, avocado, lemon juice, and all but about 4 tablespoons of the cheese. (3) Follow Step 3 above.

TIP: *In Step 2, the tomato creates a pink-colored juice which makes the outside of the chicken pieces appear undercooked. To avoid overcooking the chicken and making it tough, test the chicken by removing a piece, holding it under good light, and pulling it open to see the center, which should be white, not pink.*

TIP: *When baking in a conventional oven, large potatoes take an extra 10 minutes or so to cook.*

TIP: *To lower the fat content, substitute low-fat mozzarella and cut back on or eliminate the avocado.*

CHICKEN AND BROCCOLI TORTILLAS

Save the stem ends from fresh broccoli to make this healthful and economical tortilla entree. Tortillas toasted over a gas stove or in a cast-iron skillet are especially nice, but you can do quite well, and save some cleanup, with the microwave oven.

Preparation time: 20 minutes
Cooking time: 10 minutes
Serves: 4

1 tablespoon fresh lemon juice
1 tablespoon oil
⅛ teaspoon cayenne
2 whole chicken breasts (4 halves), skinned and boned
1 cup (from 1 bunch) broccoli stems, lightly peeled and julienned
8 8-inch flour tortillas
1 cup chopped, seeded tomato
1 green onion, white portion and first 2 inches of green, chopped
¾ cup homemade or prepared salsa
¼ cup chopped fresh coriander (cilantro)

1. Mix lemon juice, oil, and cayenne in a small bowl. Turn chicken several times in this marinade and let sit in bowl 5 minutes.
2. Drop broccoli into boiling, salted water; cook 2–3 minutes, until crisp-tender. Drain.
3. Heat broiler. Put chicken onto a lightly oiled broiler pan. Broil, turning once, 4–5 minutes, until juices run clear. Cut into strips.
4. To toast flour tortillas directly over a gas burner, heat a cast-iron skillet until hot. Add tortillas, one at a time, to the dry skillet. Cook until lightly toasted on both sides. Keep tortillas warm by wrapping in a clean towel.
5. Fill center of each tortilla evenly with chicken, broccoli, tomato, onion, and salsa. Sprinkle with coriander. Fold over bottom of tortilla, then sides.

MICROWAVE OVEN METHOD—7 minutes: (1) Follow Step 1. (2) Put broccoli, ½ teaspoon salt, and ¼ cup water in a 1-quart casserole. Cover. MICROWAVE (high) 2–3 minutes, until just tender. Drain. (3) Put chicken on a plate with thickest portions to the outside. Cover with plastic wrap, vented. MICROWAVE (high) 4–6 minutes, until center of chicken is no longer pink, turning over once. Drain. Cut into thin strips. (4) Put tortillas between damp paper towels. MICROWAVE (high) 30 seconds to 1 minute, until warm. (5) Follow Step 5.

TIP: Tortillas purchased in a plastic bag may be microwaved on high 1 or 2 minutes right in the bag. Puncture bag first a couple times with a knife or fork.

CABBAGE-CHICKEN PAPRIKA

This creamy-tart mixture of chicken and cabbage benefits from a dose of good Hungarian paprika.

Preparation time: 25 minutes
Cooking time: 25 minutes
Serves: 4

1 tablespoon oil
½ cup chopped onion
1 teaspoon minced garlic
4 chicken thighs, skinned, boned, and cubed
½ medium (2-pound) cabbage, cored and cut into ¼-inch slices (about 5 cups)
½ cup apple juice or beer
¼ teaspoon dried rosemary, crushed
½ teaspoon salt
1 tablespoon paprika, preferably imported sweet
1 tablespoon flour
1 cup sour cream
Hot, cooked noodles, about 12 ounces

1. Heat oil in a 4-quart saucepan. Add onion and garlic. Sauté 1 minute. Add chicken; sauté 5 minutes, until chicken is no longer pink.
2. Stir in cabbage, cook, covered, 5 minutes, until cabbage softens. Add remaining ingredients, except sour cream and noodles. Cook, covered, 15 minutes, stirring often, until cabbage is tender.
3. Remove from heat. Stir in sour cream. Serve over noodles.

TIP: Cabbage can be stored, wrapped in plastic in the refrigerator, for up to two weeks. Remove the two or three tough outer leaves before cooking. Wash just before using.

CHICKEN STROGANOFF

Fresh mushrooms and chicken are cooked until tender, then enriched with a sour cream-and-wine sauce. Serve over noodles.

Preparation time: 15 minutes
Cooking time: 10 minutes
Serves: 4

1 tablespoon butter
1 tablespoon olive oil
½ cup chopped onion
1 teaspoon minced fresh garlic
½ pound fresh mushrooms, sliced
2 whole chicken breasts (4 halves), skinned, boned, and cut into ½-inch-wide strips
2 teaspoons minced fresh basil *or* ½ teaspoon dried
Dash grated fresh or dried nutmeg
½ teaspoon salt
¼ teaspoon freshly ground black pepper
¼ cup dry white wine
2 tablespoons flour
2 tablespoons cold water
1 cup sour cream or sour half-and-half
2 tablespoons chopped parsley

1. Heat butter and olive oil in a 12-inch, nonstick skillet. Sauté onion and garlic 1 minute. Add mushrooms. Sauté 3–5 minutes, until golden. Add chicken and basil. Sauté about 4 minutes, until centers of chicken pieces are no longer pink.
2. Add nutmeg, salt, pepper, and wine. Boil 1 minute. Mix flour and water in a cup; stir into chicken mixture and cook 1–2 more minutes, until thickened. Remove from heat and stir in sour cream. Sprinkle with chopped parsley.

MICROWAVE OVEN METHOD—9 minutes: (1) Eliminate butter and oil. Put onion and garlic in a 2½-quart casserole. Cover. MICROWAVE (high) 1–2 minutes to start to soften. Stir in mushrooms. Cover. MICROWAVE 4–6 minutes, until mushrooms soften. (2) Arrange chicken around outer edges on top of vegetables. Cover. MICROWAVE (high) 3–4 minutes, until centers of chicken pieces are no longer pink, rearranging once. Stir in basil, nutmeg, salt, pepper, and wine. Do not cover. MICROWAVE (high) 1–2 minutes to heat, but not boil, stirring once. Eliminate flour and water. Stir in sour cream. Sprinkle with parsley.

TIP: When reheating conventionally or in the microwave oven, stir frequently, taking care to avoid boiling the dish or the sauce will curdle. When microwaving, use low power, stirring the stroganoff several times.

LIMEY CHICKEN AND PLANTAIN

The plantain, a close relative of the sweet banana, is a staple food of the tropics where it is typically paired with fish or chicken and lime. This microwave dish is very easy, because the plantain and chicken are cooked together on the same plate for the same amount of time. For added interest, we sprinkle a little fresh coriander over both.

Preparation time: 5 minutes
Microwave time: 8 minutes
Serves: 4

1 black-ripe plantain
8 chicken drumsticks, or other chicken parts, skinned
2 tablespoons lime juice
2 tablespoons minced fresh coriander (cilantro)

1. Peel plantain (use a knife, if necessary). Slice in half lengthwise, then cut into four strips. Arrange strips cut side down in single layer in center of a dinner plate.
2. Arrange chicken around plantain, with thickest portions to the outside, bones pointing in. Drizzle chicken and plantain with lime juice. Cover with plastic wrap, vented. MICROWAVE (high) 4–5 minutes, until plantain is yellow-orange and chicken is no longer pink in the center, turning the chicken pieces over once. Let stand 5 minutes. Drain. Sprinkle with coriander.

TIP: *Don't let the color of the plantain fool you. The skin turns from green to yellow and finally to black before the plantain is fully ripened. This takes about a week, at room temperature. Inside, the light-yellow fruit remains firm and gets sweeter as the skin darkens. Once cooked, ripe plantain turns a light, golden orange and tastes much like a banana.*

TIP: *If the plantain and chicken won't fit on one plate, cook them separately. Arrange the plantain cut side down on a plate, drizzle with lime juice, and cover with plastic wrap, vented. MICROWAVE (high) 3–4 minutes, until plantain is just tender and deepens to a yellow-orange color. Let stand 2 minutes. For the chicken pieces, follow Step 2.*

CHICKEN LIVERS AND MUSHROOMS

Livers and mushrooms are cooked separately to keep the flavors distinct, then gently mixed with a touch of cream and tarragon.

Preparation time: 15 minutes
Cooking time: 15 minutes
Serves: 4

1 pound chicken livers, cut in half
¼ cup finely chopped onion
½ pound mushrooms, quartered
2 tablespoons butter or margarine
2 tablespoons whipping cream
2 teaspoons fresh tarragon *or* ½ teaspoon dried
½ teaspoon salt
¼ teaspoon freshly ground black pepper
2 teaspoons lemon juice
2 green onions, white portion and first 2 inches of green, sliced

1. Rinse chicken livers under cold water and pat dry. Set aside.
2. Put onion, mushrooms, and 1 tablespoon of the butter in a large skillet. Cook and stir over medium heat 5 minutes, until onion is golden.
3. Push mushroom mixture to the edge of the skillet. Add remaining butter. When hot, add livers. Sauté 3–5 minutes, until centers of livers are no longer pink and edges are brown.
4. Stir in cream, tarragon, salt, and pepper. Cook and stir over medium heat 3 minutes, until slightly thickened. Add lemon juice. Sprinkle with green onions.

MICROWAVE OVEN METHOD—11 minutes: (1) Follow Step 1. (2) Put onion, mushrooms, and 1 tablespoon of the butter in a 2½-quart casserole. Cover with lid or plastic wrap, vented. MICROWAVE (high) 5–7 minutes, until tender, stirring once. (3) Put remaining butter on a microwave-proof plate. MICROWAVE (high) 1–2 minutes to melt. Stir in livers and arrange along rim of plate. Cover with waxed paper. MICROWAVE (medium) 4–6 minutes, until centers of livers are no longer pink. (Note that the livers are covered with waxed paper and cooked on medium—not high—power so that the thin membranes of the livers don't burst.) (4) Add livers to mushrooms. Stir in cream, tarragon, salt, and pepper. MICROWAVE (medium) 1–2 minutes, to warm. Stir in lemon juice. Top with green onions.

OVEN-CRISP CHICKEN

This oven-made dish is a more healthful alternative to fried chicken. You can even remove the skin before cooking because the freshly made bread crumbs provide the crunch. Eat these chicken pieces hot or cold.

Preparation time: 20 minutes
Cooking time: 45 minutes
Serves: 4

1 **2-pound fryer chicken, cut into 8 pieces**
2 **eggs**
2 **tablespoons milk**
4 **tablespoons (½ stick) butter**
1 **garlic clove, peeled and gently smashed**
5 **pieces whole-wheat bread**
1 **teaspoon salt**
¼ **teaspoon freshly ground black pepper**
¼ **cup sesame seeds**

1. Heat oven to 375°F. Remove skin from chicken breast, legs, and thighs; rinse and pat dry. Whisk the eggs and milk in a large bowl; add the chicken.
2. Melt the butter on a plate in the microwave oven on high power for 1 minute, or in a small saucepan over medium heat, then pour onto a plate; stir in the garlic. Set aside for a couple of minutes.
3. Toast the bread, then put in a food processor. Process to medium-fine crumbs. Add salt, pepper, and sesame seeds. Put in a shallow plate.
4. Remove the garlic from the butter. Letting the egg mixture drip off the chicken, dip each chicken piece into the butter, then into the bread-crumb mixture, patting to help crumbs stick. Arrange chicken in a nonstick, 13" × 9" baking pan. Pour any excess butter in bottom of pan, if desired. Bake 45–50 minutes, until outside of chicken is golden and the center is no longer pink.

WHOLE ROAST CHICKEN WITH BUTTERMILK GRAVY

Roast chicken needs little more than a touch of thyme, salt, and pepper—and maybe a bit of homemade gravy.

Preparation time: 15 minutes
Cooking time: 1 hour 20 minutes
Serves: 4

1 3- to 3½-pound fryer
1 tablespoon fresh thyme *or*
   1 teaspoon dried
½ teaspoon salt
⅛ teaspoon freshly ground black
   pepper
1 tablespoon olive oil

GRAVY
2 tablespoons fat from pan
   juices or 2 tablespoons butter
¾ cup Basic Chicken Stock (see
   Index) or chicken broth
2 tablespoons flour
¼ cup buttermilk or plain
   yogurt
Salt and freshly ground black
   pepper

1. Heat oven to 375°F. Remove liver and neck from fryer and reserve for another use. Rinse chicken well with cold water and pat dry. Sprinkle cavity with thyme, salt, and pepper.
2. Use a trussing needle to sew both cavities closed. Put chicken into a nonstick or lightly oiled baking pan, breast side down. Drizzle with oil. Bake 30 minutes. Turn breast side up; bake 45 more minutes, until instant thermometer registers 170°F and juices run clear.
3. Place chicken on a platter; keep warm while chicken temperature rises to 180°F. Pour pan juices into a 2-cup glass measure. Remove all but 2 tablespoons fat. Add Basic Chicken Stock to measure 1 cup. Stir in flour until smooth. Pour back into pan from chicken. Cook over medium heat about 3 minutes, until gravy is thick and smooth, stirring constantly.
4. Remove from heat. Stir a tablespoon of hot gravy into the buttermilk. Add buttermilk to gravy. Taste. Add salt and pepper—and an extra pinch of thyme—as desired.

TIP: Do not let gravy boil after buttermilk is added or the gravy will curdle. Adding the tablespoon of hot gravy to the buttermilk helps even the temperature and prevent curdling.

MICROWAVED WHOLE CHICKEN

It takes only 30 minutes to cook a whole fryer chicken when you do most of the cooking in a microwave oven, then finish the chicken (which will have a light golden skin) in the conventional oven to crisp and brown the skin.

Preparation time: 15 minutes
Microwave time: 20 minutes
Conventional oven time: 10 minutes
Serves: 4

1 **3- to 3½- pound fryer**
1 **tablespoon fresh thyme** *or* 1 **teaspoon dried**
½ **teaspoon salt**
⅛ **teaspoon freshly ground black pepper**

1. Remove liver and neck from fryer and reserve for another use. Rinse chicken well with cold water and pat dry. Sprinkle cavity with thyme, salt, and pepper.
2. Use a trussing needle to sew both cavities closed. Place chicken in a 3-quart, microwave and conventional ovenproof flat casserole, breast side down. MICROWAVE (high) 10–12 minutes to start cooking. Turn chicken over (breast side up). Cover wing tips and ends of legs with smooth strips of aluminum foil to keep them from overcooking. Pour off any juices and reserve for stocks or gravy.
3. Preheat conventional oven to 400°F.
4. MICROWAVE (high) 10–12 minutes, until instant thermometer registers 170°F. Pour off remaining juices and reserve.
5. Put chicken and baking dish in the conventional oven for about 10 minutes, until the chicken is crisp and brown. Let stand, covered with foil wrap, 10 minutes, until thermometer registers 180°F.

TIP: It's OK to use foil wrap in most microwave ovens if you keep the foil smooth and at least one inch away from the sides of the oven.

CAPON WITH MUSHROOM-PECAN DRESSING

Capons (castrated male chickens) are larger and meatier than regular fryers, and one makes a fine meal for six people. Although a smaller fryer cooks well at a high temperature (375°F or 400°F in the conventional oven, or on high power in the microwave oven), I find that larger birds such as capons cook more evenly at a medium heat (325°F in the conventional oven, or medium power in the microwave oven). The microwave oven version takes only half as long as the conventional oven method, but you need to include a short stint in the conventional oven at the end to help the skin get a little golden.

Preparation time: 30 minutes
Cooking time: 2 hours
Serves: 6

1 6- to 7-pound capon
½ cup minced onion
½ cup minced celery
4 tablespoons (½ stick) butter
½ cup chopped pecans, toasted
¼ pound (1 cup) chopped mushrooms
4 cups plain croutons
¼ cup chopped fresh parsley
1 tablespoon chopped fresh sage *or* 1 teaspoon dried
1 tablespoon chopped fresh thyme *or* 1 teaspoon dried
Salt and freshly ground black pepper
1¼ cups Basic Chicken Stock (see Index) or chicken broth

1. Heat oven to 325°F. Remove liver and neck from capon and reserve for another use. Rinse capon well with cold water and pat dry. Set aside.
2. Put onion, celery, and butter in a 3-quart saucepan. Cook and stir 4 minutes, until celery softens. Mix in pecans, mushrooms, croutons, parsley, sage, thyme, salt, and pepper.
3. Put 1 cup Basic Chicken Stock in a small saucepan. Heat to boil. Stir into pecan mixture.
4. Lightly stuff mixture into cavities of capon. Use a trussing needle to sew both cavities closed. Put capon, breast side up, in a shallow roasting pan. Roast, basting often with additional ¼ cup stock plus pan juices, 1½–2 hours, until instant thermometer registers 170°F. Let stand, covered with foil wrap, 10 minutes, until thermometer registers 180°F.

MICROWAVE OVEN METHOD—1 hour: (1) Follow Step 1. (2) Put onion, celery, and butter in a 3-quart microwave and conventional ovenproof casserole. Cover with plastic wrap, vented. MICROWAVE (high) 3–4 minutes, until celery softens. Mix in pecans, mushrooms, croutons, parsley, sage, thyme, salt, and pepper. (3) Put 1 cup Basic Chicken Stock in a 2-cup measure. (Eliminate the extra ¼ cup stock.) MICROWAVE (high) 2–3 minutes, until boiling. Stir into pecan mixture. (4) Lightly stuff mixture into cavities of capon. Use a trussing needle to sew both cavities closed. Rinse casserole clean and place capon in it, breast side down. MICROWAVE (high) 10–12 minutes to start cooking. Turn capon over (breast side up). Cover wing tips and ends of legs with smooth strips of aluminum foil to keep them from overcooking. (5) MICROWAVE (medium) 35–45 minutes, until instant-read thermometer registers 170°F. About 10 minutes before capon should be ready, preheat conventional oven to 400°F. (6) Put capon and baking dish in the conventional oven for about 10 minutes, until the capon is crisp and brown. Let stand, covered with foil wrap, 10 minutes, until thermometer registers 180°F.

TIP: *It's OK to use foil wrap in most microwave ovens if you keep the foil smooth and at least 1 inch away from the sides of the oven.*

TURKEY BREAST WITH ORANGE-CRANBERRY SAUCE

You'll find that you eat healthful turkey more often if you keep the turkey size small and the recipe simple. Here, half a turkey breast—enough for six servings—and a generous side dish of orange- and lemon-spiked fresh cranberry sauce are ready in an hour. Or, if you're in a hurry, use the microwave technique for a real meal in less than 20 minutes.

Preparation time: 15 minutes
Cooking time: 1 hour
Serves: 6

2 cups (10 ounces) fresh or frozen cranberries
2 tablespoons grated, minced orange rind
½ cup orange juice
1 tablespoon grated, minced lemon rind
2 tablespoons fresh lemon juice
¾ cup sugar
1 2-pound turkey breast half, boned
1 tablespoon olive oil
¼ teaspoon dried sage
¼ teaspoon dried thyme
¼ teaspoon dried marjoram
⅛ teaspoon freshly ground black pepper

1. Heat oven to 350°F. Mix cranberries, orange rind, orange juice, lemon rind, lemon juice, and sugar in a 2-quart saucepan. Cook over medium-low heat about 10 minutes, stirring constantly, until cranberries pop open and sauce thickens. Set aside.

2. Use a veal pounder or cleaver to briefly pound turkey breast into an even thickness. Place skin side up in a nonstick baking pan. Drizzle with oil and sprinkle with herbs and pepper. Bake 50–60 minutes, until inserted thermometer registers 170°F. Let stand on counter, lightly covered with foil, about 10 minutes, until temperature registers 180°F. Serve with orange-cranberry sauce.

MICROWAVE OVEN METHOD—17 minutes: (1) Mix cranberries, orange rind, orange juice, lemon rind, lemon juice, and sugar in a 2-quart casserole. Cover with waxed paper. MICROWAVE (high) 5–7 minutes, until cranberries pop open and sauce thickens, stirring twice. Set aside. (2) Use a veal pounder or cleaver to briefly pound turkey breast into an even thickness. Place skin side down in a 2-quart flat casserole. Eliminate olive oil. Sprinkle with herbs and pepper. Cover with plastic wrap, vented. MICROWAVE (medium) 12–16 minutes, until instant thermometer registers 170°F, turning breast over once. Let stand on counter, lightly covered with foil, about 10 minutes, until temperature registers 180°F. Serve with orange-cranberry sauce.

TIP: *Orange-cranberry sauce can be made ahead and served cold.*

TIP: *Although chicken breasts cook beautifully in the microwave oven on high power, I like to switch to medium power for a large turkey breast to help promote even, moist results.*

WHOLE TURKEY WITH APPLE-WALNUT DRESSING

A golden turkey with an old-fashioned bread stuffing makes even non-holidays seem festive. Turkeys larger than 12 pounds work best in a conventional oven. If you have a 10- to 12-pound turkey and are short on time, look to Microwaved Whole Turkey (see Index).

You can cook the turkey with or without stuffing; for health-safety reasons just be sure not to add the stuffing until right before cooking.

Preparation time: 30 minutes
Cooking time: 3½–4 hours
Serves: 8–10

⅓ **cup minced onion**
8 **tablespoons (1 stick) butter**
4 **cups dry bread cubes**
1 **small tart apple (Granny Smith is good), cored and chopped**
½ **cup chopped walnuts**
¼ **cup chopped fresh parsley**
1 **tablespoon chopped fresh sage** *or* ½ **teaspoon dried**
1 **tablespoon chopped fresh thyme** *or* ½ **teaspoon dried**
½ **teaspoon salt**
¼ **teaspoon freshly ground black pepper**
1 **cup Basic Chicken Stock (see Index) or chicken broth**
1 **egg, lightly beaten**
1 **10- to 12-pound turkey, fresh or defrosted**

1. Heat oven to 325°F. Put onion and half the butter (¼ cup) in a 3-quart saucepan. Cook and stir 3–4 minutes, until onion is tender. Stir in bread cubes, apple, walnuts, parsley, sage, thyme, salt, and pepper.
2. Put Basic Chicken Stock in a small saucepan. Heat to boil. Stir into bread mixture. Stir in egg.
3. Remove neck and wrapped innards from turkey and reserve for another use. Rinse turkey inside and out with cold water and pat dry. Lightly stuff cavities with stuffing (about 4 cups). Use a trussing needle to sew both cavities closed.
4. Melt remaining ¼ cup butter in a small saucepan. Place turkey breast side up in a shallow roasting pan. Brush with butter. Do not cover. Roast 3½–4 hours, or according to roasting times Tip below. Baste often with pan juices and butter. Let stand 15 minutes before carving.

TIP: Approximate roasting times at 325°F: 8–12 pounds = 3½–4 hours; 12–16 pounds = 4–4½ hours; 16–20 pounds = 4½–5 hours.

TIP: *Pop-up thermometers don't always work well. For doneness, rely on an instant meat thermometer. Take the bird out when the meatiest portion registers 170°F; during standing time it will rise to the recommended 180–185°F.*

TIP: *Double the dressing if using a larger bird or if your crowd loves dressing. Any dressing that doesn't fit in the turkey should be baked in a buttered baking dish at 325°F for 30 minutes, or until heated through.*

MICROWAVED WHOLE TURKEY WITH APPLE-WALNUT DRESSING

A whole turkey ready in 1½ hours? No problem with a microwave oven. This is not the way to cook a 20-pound bird—save that big one for your conventional oven. But a 10- to 12-pound turkey comes out just fine, with moist meat and a light-golden skin.

You can cook the turkey with or without stuffing; for health-safety reasons just be sure not to add the stuffing until right before cooking.

Use a pan large enough to catch the turkey drippings. And use a bulb or spoon to collect the juices so that the microwaves are attracted to the turkey, not the liquid.

For more even results, I find it best to cook turkey on medium-high power.

Preparation time: 30 minutes
Microwave time: 1½ hours
Serves: 8–10

⅓ **cup minced onion**
8 **tablespoons (1 stick) butter**
4 **cups dry bread cubes**
1 **small tart apple (Granny Smith is good), cored and chopped**
½ **cup chopped walnuts**
¼ **cup chopped fresh parsley**
1 **tablespoon chopped fresh sage** *or* ½ **teaspoon dried**
1 **tablespoon chopped fresh thyme** *or* ½ **teaspoon dried**
½ **teaspoon salt**
¼ **teaspoon freshly ground black pepper**
1 **cup Basic Chicken Stock (see Index) or chicken broth**
1 **egg, lightly beaten**
1 **10- to 12-pound turkey, fresh or defrosted**

1. Put onion and half the butter (½ stick) in a 3-quart casserole. Cover tightly with plastic wrap, vented. MICROWAVE (high) 3–4 minutes, until tender. Stir in bread cubes, apple, walnuts, parsley, sage, thyme, salt, and pepper.
2. Put Basic Chicken Stock in a 2-cup measure. MICROWAVE (high) 3–4 minutes, until boiling. Stir into bread mixture. Stir in egg.
3. Remove neck and wrapped innards from turkey and reserve for another use. Rinse turkey inside and out with cold water and pat dry. Lightly stuff cavities with stuffing (about 4 cups). Use string or plastic ties to tie both cavities closed.
4. Place remaining ½ stick butter in a 1-cup measure and MICROWAVE (high) 1–2 minutes to melt. Place turkey, breast side down, in a 3-quart flat casserole. Brush with butter. Do not cover. MICROWAVE (medium-high) 40–45 minutes, brushing with butter and collecting pan juices twice.

5. Turn turkey over (breast side up).
   MICROWAVE (medium-high) 40–45 minutes,
   until juices run clear, basting with butter and
   collecting pan juices several times. Cover
   lightly with foil wrap and let stand 15 minutes
   to finish cooking.

TIP: After the turkey has been turned to breast side up and cooked for 20 minutes, check for fast-cooking spots. If the more exposed wing tips, top of breast, and the joint between the leg and thigh are cooking faster than the rest, cover them loosely with foil wrap. Position the bird to keep the foil at least 2 inches from the microwave oven walls and continue cooking.

If you put the foil on too soon and the bird isn't cooked enough, remove the foil and continue cooking until the juices run clear.

If you put the foil on too late and portions are overcooked, trim away these dry portions before serving. The rest of the turkey will be fine.

TIP: Pop-up thermometers don't always work well in a microwave oven. For doneness, rely on an instant meat thermometer. Take the bird out when the meatiest portion registers 170°F; during standing time it will rise to the recommended 180–185°F.

COMPANY'S COMING

The recipes in this chapter are not necessarily complicated. But they often use ingredients identified with special meals: blue cheese, macadamia nuts, watercress, pine nuts, passion fruit—and butter. I love butter. Our whole family has cut way back on the amount of butter that we eat, but sometimes it's just time for a plunge back into delicious bad habits.

Flavors in this chapter may be assertive and presentations more dramatic. The final criterion is that the dishes taste great—a meal fit for company.

PINE NUT–STUFFED CHICKEN BREASTS

Stuffed, sliced chicken breasts are not as complicated to make as they look, and the neat little packages can be prepared several hours or even a day ahead. Serve with a tomato coulis *or a moist accompaniment such as creamed spinach.*

Preparation time: 40 minutes
Cooking time: 25 minutes
Serves: 4–6

2 **whole large chicken breasts (4 halves), skinned and boned**
3 **tablespoons olive oil**
3 **tablespoons butter**
2 **teaspoons minced garlic**
¼ **cup minced onion**
½ **cup chopped mushrooms**
½ **cup fine bread crumbs**
¼ **cup pine nuts**
3 **tablespoons minced fresh parsley**
2 **teaspoons chopped fresh thyme** *or* ½ **teaspoon dried**
½ **teaspoon chopped fresh oregano** *or* ⅛ **teaspoon dried**
¼ **teaspoon salt**
⅛ **teaspoon freshly ground black pepper**
3 **tablespoons flour on a plate**
¼ **cup Basic Chicken Stock (see Index) or chicken broth**
1 **tablespoon flour dissolved in ¼ cup water, whipping cream, or milk**
1 **teaspoon Worcestershire sauce**

1. Remove all fat from chicken breasts and cut away any pieces of membrane. Rinse and pat dry. Place between two pieces of waxed paper and use a veal pounder or the side of a cleaver to pound each breast gently to flatten about ⅛-inch thick. Set aside.
2. Heat 1 tablespoon each oil and butter in a large (10-inch), ovenproof skillet. Add garlic, onion, and mushrooms. Cook and stir over medium heat 3 minutes, until soft. Transfer to a small bowl. Stir in bread crumbs, pine nuts, 2 tablespoons of the parsley, thyme, oregano, salt, and pepper.
3. Heat oven to 350°F. Divide pine-nut mixture into four equal portions. Spread over four chicken breast halves; roll chicken jelly-roll fashion. Tie in several places with kitchen string or secure with poultry pins.
4. Lightly dredge rolls in flour on a plate. Shake off excess. Heat remaining 2 tablespoons each oil and butter in the same skillet until hot. Add chicken rolls. Brown on all sides, about 5 minutes. Add Basic Chicken Stock to pan. Cover, put in oven, and bake 15 minutes, until chicken juices run clear. Remove chicken to a serving plate; keep warm.

5. Put skillet over medium heat. Whisk in dissolved flour; cook and stir 3 minutes, until smooth and thick. Stir in Worcestershire sauce. Taste and adjust salt and pepper. Cut each stuffed chicken breast into 1-inch slices and arrange attractively on serving dishes. Pour sauce over chicken.

TIP: If a small strip of chicken comes loose from the main chicken breast while pounding, overlap and pound together.

PASSION FRUIT CHICKEN

Exotic passion fruit, which looks like a large, dimpled, brittle prune, adds a delicious, tropical flavor to this very simple dish.

Preparation time: 5 minutes
Cooking time: 10 minutes
Serves: 4

2 whole chicken breasts (4 halves), skinned and boned
½ cup Basic Chicken Stock (see Index) or chicken broth
1 tablespoon lemon juice
2 tablespoons whipping cream
Strained pulp from 2 passion fruit (see Tip)
1 teaspoon sugar
Salt and white pepper to taste
2 tablespoons butter, softened
2 tablespoons chopped fresh chervil or parsley

1. Place chicken between sheets of waxed paper and pound to an even thickness.
2. Put Basic Chicken Stock and lemon juice into a large, nonstick skillet. Heat to simmer; add chicken. Cover tightly. Cook 6–8 minutes, until juices from chicken run clear. Remove chicken to a plate.
3. Boil pan juices until reduced to 1 tablespoon. Add cream. Boil until reduced again to 1 tablespoon. Whisk in strained passion fruit pulp, sugar, salt, and pepper. Boil briefly. Reduce heat to very low. Whisk in butter until just smooth. Do not boil.
4. Pour juices over chicken. Sprinkle with chervil or parsley.

TIP: Passion fruit are ripe when dimply and brittle. Cut fruit in half over a bowl to catch juices. Use a spoon to scoop out mustard-colored pulp and seeds into a small, wire-mesh strainer. Push on pulp with a wooden spoon to remove seeds.

CHICKEN KABOBS WITH YELLOW-PEPPER PUREE

Sweet yellow peppers are cooked into a healthful puree that is topped with skewers of chicken cubes.

Preparation time: 10 minutes
Cooking time: 15 minutes
Serves: 4

3 medium yellow bell peppers
¼ cup water
2 tablespoons olive oil
Dash cayenne
¼ teaspoon salt
⅛ teaspoon freshly ground white pepper
2 whole chicken breasts (4 halves), skinned, boned, and cut into 1-inch cubes
1 tablespoon melted butter
1 tablespoon lemon juice

1. Heat broiler to high or prepare charcoal grill. Seed peppers and cut into 1-inch chunks. Put peppers and water in a medium saucepan. Heat to simmer, covered. Cook, stirring often, about 10 minutes, until quite tender. Drain. Puree in a blender or food processor. Mix in olive oil, cayenne, salt, and pepper. Keep warm.

2. Skewer chicken on wooden skewers so that pieces are not touching. Drizzle with melted butter and lemon juice. Place chicken kabobs on a lightly oiled broiler pan or grill, at least 4 inches from heat source. Cook, turning often, 4–6 minutes, until centers of chicken pieces are no longer pink. To serve, spoon puree onto a plate and place chicken on top.

MICROWAVE OVEN METHOD—11 minutes: (1) Seed peppers and cut into 1-inch chunks. Put peppers and water in a 2-quart casserole. MICROWAVE (high) 8–10 minutes, until quite tender, stirring after 3 minutes. Drain. Puree in a blender or food processor. Mix in olive oil, cayenne, salt, and pepper. Keep warm. (2) Skewer chicken on wooden skewers so that pieces are not touching. Arrange in a spokelike pattern on a large plate. Eliminate butter. Drizzle with lemon juice. Cover with waxed paper. MICROWAVE (high) 3–4 minutes, until centers of chicken pieces are no longer pink, rotating skewers twice. To serve, spoon puree onto plate and place chicken on top.

TIP: Red bell peppers can be substituted for the yellow, or use a 7-ounce jar of toasted red peppers; simply drain, puree, and season.

EMPEROR'S CHICKEN

This Oriental-style dish has it all: shrimp, chicken, mushrooms, pea pods, and cashews in a ginger-sesame sauce. Note that the chicken, vegetables, and shrimp are cooked in sequence to avoid overcooking the most delicate vegetables and shrimp.

Preparation time: 20 minutes
Cooking time: 10 minutes
Serves: 6

2 teaspoons minced fresh garlic
2 teaspoons minced fresh ginger
2 tablespoons soy sauce
2 tablespoons dry white wine
½ teaspoon sesame oil
¼ teaspoon freshly ground black pepper
1 whole chicken breast (2 halves), skinned, boned, and cut into 1-inch by 2-inch strips
3 tablespoons vegetable oil
½ pound fresh mushrooms, quartered
½ pound bok choy, white portion only, cut into ¼-inch diagonal slices
¼ pound snow peas, ends trimmed, top and bottom threads removed
½ pound raw medium shrimp, shelled and deveined
2 teaspoons cornstarch, dissolved in 2 tablespoons water
⅓ cup dry-roasted unsalted cashews or peanuts
2 green onions, white portion and first 2 inches of green, sliced
4 cups cooked rice

1. Mix garlic, ginger, soy sauce, wine, sesame oil, and pepper in a small bowl. Stir in chicken and let marinate 15 minutes. Place all ingredients near the stove.
2. Heat wok or a large skillet until hot. Heat vegetable oil until hot but not smoking. Add mushrooms and bok choy; stir-fry 2 minutes. Add snow peas; stir-fry 1–2 minutes, until vegetables are crisp-tender. Remove with a slotted spoon to a large plate.
3. Reheat oil in wok if necessary. Add chicken mixture; stir-fry 2 minutes. Add shrimp; stir-fry 2–3 minutes, until centers of chicken pieces are no longer pink and shrimp are just pink. Stir in cornstarch mixture. Stir-fry until mixture thickens. Sprinkle with cashews and green onions. Serve over rice.

TIP: *To butterfly the shrimp, clean as usual. Then use a small knife to cut about ¼-inch along the back edge, stopping at the tail. Press shrimp body flat. When the shrimp cook, they will curl into a butterfly shape.*

CHICKEN AND MUSHROOMS UNDER BLUE CHEESE

This beautiful dish is simpler than it appears. A basic white sauce quickly turns into a blue-cheese sauce. Fresh mushrooms cook up with little attention. And the chicken breasts are ready in a fast 6 minutes. Assemble—and enjoy your company.

Preparation time: 15 minutes
Cooking time: 15 minutes
Serves: 4

5 tablespoons butter
3 tablespoons flour
1 cup milk, at room temperature
¼ teaspoon salt
⅛ teaspoon freshly ground black pepper
3 ounces blue cheese, crumbled
2 cups finely chopped mushrooms
¼ cup finely chopped onion
2 whole chicken breasts (4 halves), skinned, boned, and pounded flat
2 tablespoons minced fresh parsley

1. Melt 3 tablespoons of the butter in a small saucepan. Stir in flour; cook and stir 1 minute over medium heat. Whisk in milk, salt, and pepper. Cook 3 minutes, stirring constantly, until smooth and thick. Remove from heat. Stir in cheese until melted.

2. Melt remaining 2 tablespoons butter in a 12-inch, nonstick skillet. Stir in mushrooms and onion; cook and stir over medium heat 5 minutes, until onion is golden. Move mushroom mixture to edge of skillet. Add chicken in a single layer. Brown both sides of the chicken, about 3 minutes. (Cook in batches if pan is not large enough.) Put all chicken in the skillet. Cook, covered, 3 minutes, until juices run clear.

3. Place chicken on a serving plate. Spread mushroom mixture evenly on the chicken. Reheat sauce if necessary (see Tip). Spoon over chicken. Sprinkle with parsley.

TIP: The sauce (Step 1) can be made ahead, covered, and refrigerated. Rewarm carefully over low heat. Add a little milk if it gets too thick.

TOMATOES STUFFED WITH CHICKEN AND CHEVRE

Fresh, tangy goat cheese adds wonderful zip to these stuffed tomatoes. Note that the chicken filling is cooked first, then the stuffed tomatoes are broiled to allow the filling to heat through before the shells get too soft.

Preparation time: 20 minutes
Cooking time: 10 minutes
Serves: 4

4 medium to large tomatoes
Salt
¼ cup minced onion
2 tablespoons olive oil
1 whole chicken breast (2 halves), skinned, boned, and cubed
2½ cups fresh bread cubes
½ teaspoon salt
¼ teaspoon freshly ground black pepper
¼ cup loosely packed chopped fresh basil *or* 2 teaspoons dried
3 ounces soft, mild chèvre (Montrachet is a fine choice)
Chopped fresh parsley or chives

1. Heat broiler to high. Slice ½ inch off the tops of the tomatoes. Remove cores of flesh and seeds, leaving thick, meaty shells. Discard seeds; chop inner flesh and reserve. Sprinkle shells lightly with salt. Set tomato shells upside down to drain.
2. Put onion and olive oil in a medium, nonstick skillet. Cook and stir over medium heat 2 minutes. Add chicken; cook 4–5 minutes, until centers of chicken pieces are no longer pink. Remove from heat.
3. Lightly mix in ¼ cup reserved tomato flesh, bread cubes, salt, pepper, basil, and chèvre. Taste mixture; adjust seasoning to taste.
4. Fill tomato shells with chèvre mixture. Put into a shallow baking pan or broiler pan lined with foil. Broil at least 4 inches from heat source, about 3 minutes, until heated through and tops are slightly golden. Sprinkle with parsley or chives.

CHICKEN MORNAY

Mornay sauce—a white sauce with cheese—is a snap to make. Because both the chicken and sauce are light in color, we slip them under the broiler with a little extra cheese to brown lightly before serving.

Preparation time: 10 minutes
Cooking time: 10 minutes
Broiler time: 5 minutes
Serves: 4

2 whole chicken breasts (4 halves), skinned and boned
4 tablespoons butter
2 tablespoons flour
1 cup milk
¼ teaspoon salt
⅛ teaspoon freshly ground white pepper
Dash cayenne
¼ cup plus 2 tablespoons grated Parmesan
¼ cup grated Swiss cheese or Gruyère

1. Pound chicken between sheets of waxed paper to flatten evenly. Heat 2 tablespoons of the butter in a large, nonstick skillet. Add chicken in a single layer. Brown both sides, about 3 minutes. Cook, covered, 3 minutes, until juices run clear. Remove from heat.
2. Heat broiler.
3. Melt remaining 2 tablespoons butter in a small saucepan. Stir in flour; cook and stir 1 minute over medium heat. Whisk in milk, salt, pepper, and cayenne. Cook, stirring constantly, 3 minutes, until smooth and thick. Remove from heat. Stir in ¼ cup Parmesan and the Swiss cheese or Gruyère until melted. Taste and adjust seasoning.
4. Pour sauce over chicken. Sprinkle with remaining 2 tablespoons Parmesan. Put under broiler for 2–3 minutes, or until lightly browned.

TIP: Cheese will melt better if it is finely grated.

MEDITERRANEAN CHICKEN WITH PASTA

Chicken breasts are topped with an olive-studded, homemade tomato sauce which also helps moisten the accompanying spaghetti. Imported olives make the sauce special.

Preparation time: 15 minutes
Cooking time: 35 minutes
Serves: 4

1 tablespoon olive oil
½ cup minced onion
1 tablespoon minced garlic
½ cup dry white wine
2 cups peeled, seeded, and chopped tomatoes, or 1 15-ounce can, drained
¼ cup chopped, pitted black olives
¼ cup chopped, pitted green olives
½ teaspoon capers
½ teaspoon sugar
½ cup Basic Chicken Stock (see Index) or chicken broth
1 6-ounce can tomato paste
⅛ teaspoon red pepper flakes
2 whole chicken breasts (4 halves), skinned and boned
1 pound spaghetti, cooked and drained
3 tablespoons minced fresh parsley or basil

1. Put olive oil, onion, and garlic in a 2-quart saucepan. Cook and stir 2–3 minutes to soften.
2. Stir in wine, tomatoes, black olives, green olives, capers, sugar, Basic Chicken Stock, tomato paste, and red pepper flakes. Simmer 25 minutes to thicken. Taste and adjust seasoning. Set aside and keep warm.
3. Put chicken onto a lightly oiled broiler pan. Broil, turning once, 6 minutes, until juices are no longer pink.
4. Place chicken atop spaghetti and top with sauce. Sprinkle with parsley or basil.

MICROWAVE OVEN METHOD—19 minutes: (1) Put olive oil, onion, and garlic in a 2-quart casserole. MICROWAVE (high) 2–3 minutes to soften. (2) Stir in wine, tomatoes, black olives, green olives, capers, sugar, Basic Chicken Stock, tomato paste, and red pepper flakes. MICROWAVE (high), uncovered, 13–15 minutes to thicken, stirring twice. Set aside and keep warm. (3) Put chicken on a plate with thickest portions to the outside. Cover with plastic wrap, vented. MICROWAVE (high) 4–6 minutes, until center of chicken is no longer pink, turning pieces over once. Drain. (4) Follow Step 4.

CHICKEN- AND SPINACH-STUFFED EGGPLANT

Glossy purple eggplant looks beautiful filled with this creamy chicken-and-spinach mixture. The eggplant shell—tender enough to eat—serves as a natural insulator, keeping the dish warm while you finish preparing dinner.

Preparation time: 40 minutes
Cooking time: 1 hour
Serves: 4

1 **10-ounce package frozen chopped spinach**
1 **medium eggplant**
1½ **teaspoons salt**
1 **tablespoon olive oil**
2 **tablespoons butter**
1 **cup sliced mushrooms**
3 **tablespoons chopped onion**
1 **clove garlic, minced**
1 **whole chicken breast (2 halves), skinned, boned, and cut into ½-inch cubes**
⅛ **teaspoon freshly ground black pepper**
2 **tablespoons minced fresh basil** *or* ½ **teaspoon dried**
2 **tablespoons flour dissolved in ¼ cup milk**
½ **cup Basic Chicken Stock (see Index) or chicken broth**
Chopped green onion for garnish

1. Thaw spinach. Squeeze and drain well. Set aside.
2. Cut eggplant in half lengthwise. Scoop out pulp, leaving ¼-inch-thick shells. (A grapefruit spoon works well.) Sprinkle shells generously with ½ teaspoon salt. Drain upside down on paper towels 30 minutes. Pat dry.
3. Heat oven to 350°F. Coarsely chop pulp. Heat olive oil and butter in a large skillet. Add pulp, mushrooms, onion, and garlic. Cook and stir 5 minutes, until onion is golden. Stir in chicken. Cook and stir 3 minutes, until chicken is no longer pink. Stir in spinach, 1 teaspoon salt, pepper, and basil. Cook and stir 1 minute. Stir in dissolved flour mixture. Cook and stir 2 minutes, until thick.
4. Stuff mixture into eggplant shells. Place shells in an 11″ × 7″ baking pan or casserole dish. Pour Basic Chicken Stock into pan. Bake tightly covered 40 minutes. Uncover; bake 10 more minutes. Sprinkle with green onion.

MICROWAVE OVEN METHOD—20 minutes: (1) Follow Step 1. (2) Follow Step 2. (3) Coarsely chop pulp. Mix pulp, ¼ cup water, and ¼ teaspoon salt in a 4-quart casserole. Cover. MICROWAVE (high) 3–5 minutes, until pulp is just tender. Drain. (4) Add drained spinach, olive oil, 1 tablespoon butter (eliminate the other tablespoon butter), mushrooms, onion, garlic, chicken, 1 teaspoon salt, pepper, and basil to drained eggplant. Cover. MICROWAVE (high) 6–8 minutes, until chicken is no longer pink, stirring twice. Stir in flour and cream mixture. (5) Put shells on a microwave-proof serving dish. Fill shells with mixture. Eliminate the Basic Chicken Stock. Cover with waxed paper. MICROWAVE (high) 6–7 minutes, until shell exteriors are just tender. Sprinkle with green onion.

TIP: *To carve a neat eggplant shell, first use a knife or grapefruit spoon to follow the oval shape ¼ inch within the split shell. Scoop out pulp with a spoon.*

CHICKEN DE JONGHE

Chicken is substituted for shrimp in this takeoff on shrimp de Jonghe, a butter-rich dish that dates back to Henri de Jonghe and his turn-of-the-century Chicago Loop restaurant.

Preparation time: 10 minutes
Cooking time: 10 minutes
Serves: 2–3

¼ **cup dry white wine or sherry**
1 **bay leaf, crumbled**
1 **chicken breast (2 halves), skinned, boned, and cut into 1-inch chunks**
8 **tablespoons (1 stick) butter**
1 **teaspoon lemon juice**
1 **teaspoon minced fresh garlic**
1 **tablespoon minced shallot**
2 **tablespoons minced fresh parsley**
⅛ **teaspoon cayenne**
¼ **teaspoon salt**
⅛ **teaspoon freshly ground black pepper**
½ **cup fresh, coarse French bread crumbs**

1. Heat broiler to high. Put wine, bay leaf, and chicken in a broiler-proof skillet. Cook and stir over medium-low heat 5 minutes, until centers of chicken pieces are no longer pink.
2. Melt butter in a small saucepan over low heat. Remove from heat. Stir in lemon juice, garlic, shallot, parsley, cayenne, salt, pepper, and all but 1 tablespoon of the bread crumbs.
3. Top chicken with butter–bread-crumb mixture. Sprinkle with remaining bread crumbs. Broil, 4 inches from heat source, 3–4 minutes, until bread crumbs are lightly browned.

MICROWAVE OVEN METHOD—6 minutes: (1) Put white wine, bay leaf, and chicken in a broiler- and microwave-proof 1-quart casserole (Pyrex is good). Cover. MICROWAVE (high) 2–3 minutes, until centers of chicken pieces are no longer pink, stirring once. Let stand 2 minutes. Drain, reserving 2 tablespoons liquid. (2) Put butter in a 2-cup measure. MICROWAVE (high) 1–2 minutes to melt. Stir in lemon juice, garlic, shallot, parsley, cayenne, salt, pepper, and all but 1 tablespoon of the bread crumbs. (3) Follow Step 3.

TOMATILLO CHICKEN

J. L. Franklin of Dallas got us started with this terrific, highly flavored dish enhanced with tasty green mole made with green hot peppers, pepitas (a variety of fresh pumpkin seeds), and fresh coriander. Ideally, J. L. likes to grill the chicken first before adding it to the sauce for the final cooking. However, you can make this fine dish indoors in a skillet. Serve with rice.

Preparation time: 15 minutes
Cooking time: 25 minutes
Serves: 4

½ cup unsalted pepitas (you can substitute unsalted sunflower seeds or pine nuts)
2 strips bacon, diced
8 chicken thighs, skinned and boned
2 teaspoons minced garlic
10–12 tomatillos, husked and chopped fine
2 4-ounce cans chopped green hot peppers
2 tablespoons bread crumbs
1 cup Basic Chicken Stock (see Index) or chicken broth
½ cup minced fresh coriander (cilantro)
1 lime
Salt
Cooked rice
Lime wedges

1. Put pepitas in a large (12-inch), deep, non-aluminum skillet (such as stainless steel). Place over medium heat. Cook, 3–4 minutes, until seeds pop and start to turn golden, stirring constantly at the end. Immediately remove to a plate to cool.

2. Cook bacon in the same pan over medium heat, stirring often, 3–4 minutes, until golden. Remove with a slotted spoon to a plate. Reserve. Remove all but 2 tablespoons fat from the pan. Heat until hot. Add chicken in a single layer. Cook over medium heat, turning often, 8–10 minutes, until chicken is golden and juices run clear. Remove chicken to a plate. Pour off all fat from the skillet.

3. Stir garlic, tomatillos, hot peppers, and bread crumbs into pan. Cook and stir 1 minute, scraping up brown bits from the pan bottom. Add Basic Chicken Stock and chicken and heat to a boil. Reduce heat to low; simmer uncovered 10 minutes, until thickened and flavors have blended. (Can be made ahead to this point.)

4. Stir in pepitas, coriander, and juice of half the lime. Taste and adjust salt. Serve over rice. Sprinkle with bacon. Garnish with lime wedges.

TIP: Pumpkin seeds (pepitas) are available at health food stores and Latin American markets.

TIP: You may grill or broil the chicken: boneless thighs (10–12 minutes) or boneless breasts (8–9 minutes).

ROAST DUCK

Moist, rich-tasting roast duck is almost as easy to make as roast chicken. The difference is that duck has more fat.

To decrease the amount of fat, pull excess fat from the cavity and prick the skin to help the fat escape while the duck is cooking. Be sure to use a pan large enough to hold the fat drippings—about 2 cups from a 3- to 4-pound duck.

Serve the duck with Normandy Applesauce (see Index) or substitute it for chicken in Mango Chutney Salad (see Index).

Preparation time: 10 minutes
Cooking time: 2 hours
Serves: 4

1 4½-pound duck
½ teaspoon salt
¼ teaspoon freshly ground
   black pepper
Normandy Applesauce (see
   Index)

1. Remove neck and giblets from duck and save for another use. Pull off and discard excess fat from cavity. Rinse duck well inside and out with cold water. Pat dry. Sprinkle salt and pepper in cavity. Use a fork to prick skin about every 2 inches. Close cavity with wooden picks. Use nylon string to tie legs together.
2. Heat oven to 350°F.
3. Put duck breast side up on a rack set in a roasting pan. Bake about 2 hours, until juices run clear when thigh is pricked with a fork, piercing skin often with a fork to drain off fat. Serve warm with Normandy Applesauce.

MICROWAVE OVEN METHOD—30 minutes: (1) Follow Step 1. (2) Heat conventional oven to 500°F. (3) Place duck breast side down on a microwave-safe rack (a bacon rack is fine) and place rack in a large, flat casserole. Do not cover. MICROWAVE (high) 10–12 minutes, to start cooking. Drain fat. (4) Turn duck over. MICROWAVE (high) 10–12 minutes, until juices run clear when thigh is pricked with a fork. Let stand 5 minutes. (5) Transfer duck to a conventional ovenproof broiler pan. Put in oven for about 10 minutes, until skin is lightly crisp. Serve warm with Normandy Applesauce.

TIP: When microwaving, I prefer to cook a whole duck uncovered on high power because it gives the meat a fine texture. For a softer, more stewed texture, you can cover the duck loosely with waxed paper or with plastic wrap, vented. When covered, the duck will cook faster, so turn it after 8–10 minutes, then check for doneness after another 8–10 minutes. Either way, the skin will be soft; a short stint in a very hot conventional oven helps crisp the skin lightly.

TWIN CORNISH HENS WITH APPLE STUFFING

In about 1 hour, two apple- and walnut-stuffed Cornish game hens can be ready for guests. Those with large appetites will appreciate a whole hen; I find half a hen an ample serving, especially if several side dishes also are offered. Serve with wild rice and fresh carrots.

Preparation time: 15 minutes
Cooking time: 1 hour
Serves: 2–4

2 1- to 1¾-pound Cornish game hens
¼ cup chopped onion
½ cup chopped celery
2 tablespoons butter
¾ cup cored, peeled, chopped apple (Granny Smith is good)
¼ cup chopped walnuts
1 tablespoon lemon juice
¼ cup fine, dry bread crumbs
Salt and freshly ground black pepper to taste
¼ cup currant jelly
1 teaspoon dry sherry or apple juice
1 tablespoon olive oil

1. Heat oven to 375°F. Rinse hens well with cold water and pat dry. Set aside.
2. Put onion, celery, and butter in a medium skillet. Cook and stir over medium heat 3–4 minutes, until celery softens. Mix in apple, walnuts, lemon juice, bread crumbs, salt, and pepper.
3. Put jelly and sherry or apple juice in a small saucepan. Cook over low heat, until jelly is melted. Stir. Remove from heat.
4. Lightly stuff mixture into cavities of hens. Use a trussing needle to sew cavities closed. Put into a shallow roasting pan; rub hens with oil. Cover with foil. Bake, uncovered, 30 minutes. Uncover; brush with jelly mixture. Continue baking 20–30 more minutes, basting often, until juices run clear or instant thermometer registers 170°F.
5. Let stand covered with foil wrap 10 minutes, until thermometer registers 180°F. Cut each hen in half through the breast bone and serve skin side up.

TIP: For 4 hens, double recipe; cooking time will be the same.

KID STUFF

They love carrots, but three bites are enough. Chicken is OK, as long as it's drumsticks. No food can be wrapped up and hidden—unless they do the hiding themselves.

The joys and woes of cooking for kids are as complicated as VCRs, CDs, and the clock on your first microwave oven. None of which we would be using today unless one of the kids showed us how. The microwave oven—great for easy cleanups—gets heavy use in this chapter.

The recipes in this chapter were developed for, sometimes created by, and tested on kids. If they didn't like the stuff, it didn't make this chapter. To older chaps who find the ingredients simple and repetitive, portions small, and spices bland, we say . . . look to another chapter. This one's for kids.

(In those other chapters, try Mozzarella Chicken, Raspberry-Chicken Salad, Chicken with Pea Pods, Almond Chicken and Rice, Sesame Chicken Wings, Chicken Nachos, Japanese Noodle Soup, Mom's Chicken Salad, Chicken-Stuffed Peppers, and Micro-Barbecued Chicken Pieces.)

TURKEY WITH APPLE MUSH

This recipe works like a two-ring circus: While the turkey chunks are cooking around the edge of the plate, a fresh cut-up apple in the center is turning into homemade applesauce.

Preparation time: 5 minutes
Microwave time: 3 minutes
Serves: 2

1 **apple (McIntosh is good),
  skinned, cored, and cut into
  ½-inch cubes**
6 **ounces turkey meat, skinned
  and cut into ¾-inch cubes**
1 **teaspoon brown sugar**

1. Put apple chunks in center of a microwave-proof dinner-size plate. Arrange turkey around the edges so that the turkey pieces are not touching. Cover with plastic wrap, vented. MICROWAVE (high) 3–4 minutes, until turkey pieces are no longer pink in the center, turning pieces over once. Let stand in microwave oven for 1 minute.
2. Carefully remove plastic wrap. Sprinkle sugar over apples. Use a fork or potato masher to mash the apples into applesauce, mixing in the juices on the plate.

TIP: The turkey and applesauce colors are bland, so add bright extras on the plate such as green peas, sliced beets, or carrots.

TIP: Boneless, skinned chicken may be substituted for the turkey.

FUNNY TORTILLAS

Picking your own filling for a rolled-up tortilla is more than fun—it also can be healthful eating. Below are some suggested fillings that many children enjoy; the exact amounts will vary depending on the child. The cheeses provide moisture, which is especially useful if the children don't appreciate salsa or taco sauces.

Preparation time: 15 minutes
Microwave time: 20–30 seconds for each tortilla

2–3 tortillas per child
Cooked chicken meat, sliced thin
Sliced black olives
Chopped fresh tomato
Grated fresh carrot
Sliced fresh mushrooms
Sliced green onion
Thinly sliced snow peas
Grated cheddar
Grated Parmesan
Thinly sliced mozzarella
Mild salsa or taco sauce

Arrange chicken, vegetables, cheese, and salsa in center of tortilla. Roll up tortilla and loosely wrap with paper towels. Place fold-side down on floor of microwave oven. MICROWAVE (high) 20–30 seconds, until warm. Repeat for each tortilla.

TIP: *When we were experimenting with these tortillas, cousins Ashley Tennison and Tessa Riess quickly latched onto some favorite combinations (mozzarella-Parmesan-cheddar-chicken; cheddar-olives-chicken), and discarded some otherwise favorite food items (fresh strawberries and raspberries) as too funny for Funny Tortillas. By all means, create your own renditions.*

CHICKEN MUFFIN PIZZAS

These quick pizzas—made with English muffins—make a fine lunch or afternoon snack. The chicken gets a pretty golden color and the muffin toasts nicely in the broiler. However, if you're in a hurry or are more comfortable cooking with a microwave oven, try that speedy method instead. The recipe gives instructions for starting with uncooked chicken but using leftover cooked chicken makes the pizza even faster to make.

Preparation time: 10 minutes
Cooking time: 10 minutes
Serves: 4–6

1 whole chicken breast (2 halves), skinned and boned
4 English muffins, split and toasted
1 8-ounce can (1 cup) prepared pizza sauce
1 cup grated mozzarella
1 tablespoon chopped fresh basil *or* **1 teaspoon dried**
2 teaspoons olive oil
Crushed red pepper flakes (optional)

1. Heat broiler to high. Put chicken onto an oiled broiler pan. Broil, 4 inches from the heat, 7–8 minutes, turning once, until chicken is golden and juices run clear. Cut into long, flat slices.
2. Put English muffins cut side up on a foil-lined broiler pan. Arrange chicken slices on top of each muffin. Spoon pizza sauce over chicken. Sprinkle on cheese, basil, and olive oil.
3. Broil, 4 inches from the heat, 1½–2 minutes, until cheese is golden. Serve 1 or 2 little pizzas for each person. Serve with red pepper flakes, if desired.

MICROWAVE OVEN METHOD—4 minutes: (1) Put chicken on a microwave-proof dinner plate. Cover with plastic wrap, vented. MICROWAVE (high) 2–3 minutes, until center of chicken is no longer pink, turning over once. Let stand 2 minutes to finish cooking. Drain. Cut into long, flat slices. (2) Put English muffins cut side up on a paper towel-lined plate. Arrange as in Step 2. (3) MICROWAVE (medium) 1½–2 minutes, until cheese melts. Serve with red pepper flakes, if desired. Serve 1 or 2 little pizzas for each person.

TIP: Note that the pizzas are cooked in the microwave oven on medium power, not high, to keep the cheese from cooking too fast and getting tough.

ASHLEY'S CHICKEN 'N' BISCUITS

Homemade baking-powder biscuits are a favorite Sunday breakfast that our children enjoy making—in huge numbers. With the leftover biscuits, nine-year-old Ashley created the following recipe for Sunday-night chicken and biscuits. The microwave oven is used to reheat the biscuits (they must be made in a conventional oven—the microwave just doesn't do the trick with biscuits) and to cook the chicken.

Preparation time: 5 minutes
Microwave time: 3 minutes
Serves: 2–4

1 **whole chicken breast (2 halves), skinned and boned**
4 **baking-powder biscuits**
8 **tablespoons apple butter**

1. Put chicken on a plate, with thickest portions to the outside. Cover with plastic wrap, vented. MICROWAVE (high) 2–3 minutes, until center of chicken is no longer pink, turning pieces over once. Let stand 2 minutes. Drain. Cut into thin strips.
2. Put biscuits on a paper towel–lined plate. Cover with another paper towel. MICROWAVE (medium) 1–2 minutes to heat.
3. Use knife to cut biscuits in half horizontally. Spread 1 tablespoon butter on each half. Divide chicken on the biscuit halves and top with a little more apple butter.

CHICKEN FLOWERS

"Make one of those tomato roses for the middle," said our daughter Ashley, "and use the chicken for the petals." Our chicken flower was underway.

We scoured the produce department for the right green "stem" and settled on broccoli stalks. (Fresh green beans are out of season too often. Asparagus look good, but many kids don't like them.)

Several tads more sophisticated than a clown face, this flower—made from chicken, tomato, and broccoli—is too pretty not to eat. And the microwave makes it easy to cook small portions of chicken and vegetables. The only tricky part is the tomato rose, but with a little practice even a nine-year-old can handle the chore. Truly.

Preparation time: 20 minutes
Microwave time: 5 minutes
Serves: 4

4 medium tomatoes
1 whole chicken breast
   (2 halves), skinned and boned
Stems from 1 medium stalk
   broccoli

1. To make a tomato rose: Using a small, sharp knife, start to cut a ¼-inch-thick circle about the size of a quarter on the smooth end (not the stem end) of a tomato. Instead of completing the little circle, continue cutting the skin around the tomato into one long, ¾-inch-wide strip. Save the pulpy skinned center for some other use.
2. Starting at the end (not the quarter-size circle) of the strip, roll the strip into a tight, concentric circle. When you get to the end of the strip, use the quarter-size circle as the base of the flower; set the rest of the strip on top and gently spread open into a roselike shape. Repeat with remaining tomatoes.
3. Put chicken on a plate with thickest portions to the outside. Cover with plastic wrap, vented. MICROWAVE (high) 2–3 minutes, until center of chicken is no longer pink, turning pieces over once. Let stand 2 minutes. Drain. Cut into ½-inch-wide strips, curving strips slightly to look like petals.
4. Lightly peel broccoli stems. Cut into flat, ½-inch-wide strips. (If the strips are forked,

that's even better for a stalklike look.) Put
broccoli in a 1-quart casserole with 2
tablespoons water. Cover. MICROWAVE (high)
3–4 minutes, until fork-tender. Drain.

5. To make chicken flowers, use dark-colored
plates so that the light chicken meat stands out.
Place a tomato rose in the center of the plate.
Arrange the chicken strips around the rose like
additional petals. Use the broccoli for a stem.

CHICKEN-STUFFED APPLES

Cut-up chicken breast is first thoroughly cooked, then used to stuff fresh, whole apples. Let the stuffed apples cool slightly before serving. The microwave oven does a wonderful job with this dish, and in a mere 10 minutes. If you prefer to use a conventional oven, note that you will need to add an extra ¼ cup apple juice to keep the apples moist during the longer cooking time.

Preparation time: 20 minutes
Microwave time: 10 minutes
Serves: 4

4 large, tart apples (Granny Smith are good)
1 whole chicken breast (2 halves), skinned, boned, and cut into 1-inch pieces
1½ cups chopped leek (1 medium leek)
½ teaspoon dried sage
¼ teaspoon salt
¼ teaspoon freshly ground black pepper
½ cup fresh bread cubes (1 slice bread)
2 tablespoons butter
¼ cup apple juice

1. Core and hollow out apples, leaving ½-inch shells and being sure not to cut through bottoms. Peel a thin strip around the center of each apple to keep the skins from splitting. Set apples aside.
2. Put chicken and leek in a 2-quart casserole. Cover. MICROWAVE (high) 4–5 minutes, until chicken is no longer pink, stirring twice. Stir in sage, salt, pepper, and bread cubes.
3. Stuff apples with chicken-leek mixture. Put on round dish. Top each apple with ½ tablespoon butter and 1 tablespoon apple juice.
4. Cover. MICROWAVE (high) 6–7 minutes, until apples are tender but still holding their shape, rotating dish once.

CONVENTIONAL OVEN METHOD—45 minutes: (1) Follow Step 1. (2) Heat oven to 325°F. (3) Melt 1 tablespoon of the butter in a large skillet. Add leek; cook and stir 2 minutes, until wilted. Add chicken; cook and stir 4 minutes, until golden. Stir in sage, salt, pepper, and bread cubes. (4) Stuff apples with chicken-leek mixture. Put in a baking or pie plate. Increase apple juice to ½ cup. Top each apple with ¼ tablespoon butter and 2 tablespoons apple juice. (5) Bake, covered tightly, 40 minutes, until apples are crisp-tender.

MICRO-GRILLING

Nothing can duplicate the distinct taste and texture of grilled food. But some foods—particularly chicken—seem to take forever to cook on the grill.

Here's where your microwave oven comes to the rescue. In the time that it takes for the charcoal to be ready, your chicken can be moist-cooked in the microwave oven. Stick the chicken on the grill for just a few minutes to pick up that special charcoal flavor and light grill marks. It's so easy.

And micro-grilled chicken is absolutely delicious—*better* than plain grilled because it's more moist. Plus you have the bonus of speed.

Duck, and even a whole turkey, benefit from the dual cooking method, too.

MICRO-BARBECUED CHICKEN PIECES

An American favorite, updated with the microwave oven. While the grill is heating, a whole, cut-up chicken is cooked in the microwave oven. A final few minutes on the grill adds that distinct charcoal flavor and some light grill marks.

Use your favorite barbecue sauce or this thick, lightly spiced, red-wine version, which you'll want to make ahead of time.

Preparation time: 10 minutes
Microwave time: 11 minutes
Grilling time: 10 minutes
Serves: 4

1 2- to 3-pound chicken, cut up
½ cup Red-Wine Barbecue Sauce
   (recipe follows)

1. Start grill. Place chicken legs (whole, or drumsticks and thighs) in a 13″ × 9″ casserole. Cover with plastic wrap, vented. MICROWAVE (high) 1–2 minutes to start cooking.

2. Add remaining chicken pieces: thighs and legs in corners, breasts on the sides, and wings in the middle, with the thickest portions facing the outside. Brush with sauce. Cover with plastic wrap, vented. MICROWAVE (high) 10–14 minutes, until meat is no longer pink and juices run clear, turning pieces over after 6–8 minutes. Let stand 5 minutes. Drain.

3. Place chicken pieces skin side down on grill, 6 inches from medium-hot coals. Brush with sauce. Do not cover grill. Grill for 5 minutes, turn pieces over, and brush with sauce. Grill 5 minutes. Serve with extra sauce on the side.

RED-WINE BARBECUE SAUCE

Cook the sauce down to just less than 1 cup, or until it is thick enough to coat a spoon.

Preparation time: 10 minutes
Microwave time: 14–18 minutes
Yield: almost 1 cup

½ cup finely chopped onion
1 teaspoon minced garlic
1 teaspoon olive oil
⅓ cup catsup
¾ cup dry red wine
¼ cup apple cider vinegar
1 tablespoon Worcestershire
   sauce
½ teaspoon dry mustard
1 tablespoon fresh thyme *or*
   1 teaspoon dried
⅛ teaspoon freshly ground black
   pepper

1. Put onion, garlic, and olive oil in a 2-quart casserole. Cover. MICROWAVE (high) 2–3 minutes to soften.
2. Stir in remaining ingredients. MICROWAVE (high), uncovered, 12–15 minutes, until sauce thickens.

MICRO-GRILLED SESAME BREASTS

Light-meat chicken breasts are matched with a light and sweetened vinaigrette.

Preparation time: 10 minutes
Microwave time: 7 minutes
Grilling time: 10 minutes
Serves: 4

**2 whole chicken breasts (4
halves), skin on**
½ **cup Sweet Sesame Dressing
(recipe follows)**

1. Start grill. Place chicken breasts on a plate with the thickest portions facing to the outside. Brush with dressing. Cover with plastic wrap, vented. MICROWAVE (high) 7–9 minutes, until meat is no longer pink and juices run clear, turning pieces over after 5–6 minutes. Let stand 3 minutes. Drain.
2. Place chicken pieces skin side down on grill, 6 inches from medium-hot coals. Brush with dressing. Do not cover grill. Grill for 5 minutes, turn pieces over, and brush with sauce. Grill 5 minutes. Serve with extra dressing on the side.

SWEET SESAME DRESSING

This honey-sweetened dressing makes a nice light basting sauce for chicken breasts. The microwave oven makes it easy to "toast" the sesame seeds without worrying about burning them.

Preparation time: 5 minutes
Microwave time: 3 minutes
Yield: ½ cup

2 tablespoons sesame seeds
1 teaspoon minced fresh garlic
1½ tablespoons white-wine
  vinegar
Dash red pepper flakes
⅛ teaspoon dried oregano
¼ teaspoon salt
⅛ teaspoon freshly ground
  black pepper
¼ cup vegetable oil, such as
  safflower
2 tablespoons honey

1. Put sesame seeds on a small plate and shake to spread them. MICROWAVE (high) uncovered 2–3 minutes, until well heated. Set aside.
2. Put garlic, vinegar, red pepper flakes, oregano, salt, and pepper in a 4-cup measure. MICROWAVE (high) 1–2 minutes, until garlic and dried spices are softened. Whisk in oil and honey. Add sesame seeds.

MICRO-GRILLED CHICKEN LEGS WITH OYSTER BARBECUE SAUCE

If you cook just one cut of chicken at a time—all legs or all breasts—it's easier to figure out when the chicken is fully cooked. This all-legs dish gets extra color and flavor from a little sweetened and spiced-up bottled oyster sauce.

Preparation time: 10 minutes
Microwave time: 8 minutes
Grilling time: 10 minutes
Serves: 4

4 whole chicken legs, or 4 drumsticks and 4 thighs
¼ cup Oyster Barbecue Sauce (recipe follows)

1. Start grill. Place chicken legs (whole, or drumsticks and thighs) in a 13″ × 9″ casserole with the thickest portions facing to the outside. Brush with sauce. Cover with plastic wrap, vented. MICROWAVE (high) 8–10 minutes, until meat is no longer pink and juices run clear, turning pieces over after 5–6 minutes. Let stand 5 minutes. Drain.
2. Place chicken pieces skin side down on grill, 6 inches from medium-hot coals. Brush with sauce. Do not cover grill. Grill for 5 minutes; turn pieces over and brush with sauce. Grill 5 minutes. Serve with extra sauce on the side.

OYSTER BARBECUE SAUCE

Preparation time: 10 minutes
Microwave time: 2–3 minutes
Yield: ¼ cup

½ teaspoon minced fresh garlic
½ teaspoon minced fresh ginger
¼ cup bottled oyster sauce
2 tablespoons water
1 tablespoon fresh lemon juice
2 teaspoons sugar
⅛ teaspoon dried red pepper
  flakes

Put all ingredients in a 2-cup measure.
MICROWAVE (high) 2–3 minutes, until garlic and ginger are softened. Stir well.

SPICY MUSTARD MICRO-GRILLED WINGS

These nippy wings (anchovy paste is the secret sauce ingredient) make fun appetizers.

Preparation time: 10 minutes
Microwave time: 6 minutes
Grilling time: 10 minutes
Serves: 4–6

10–12 chicken wings (2 pounds, total)
½ cup Spicy Mustard Barbecue Sauce (recipe follows)

1. Start grill. Use kitchen scissors to cut off wing tips (save for soup or discard). Place chicken wings in a single layer in a 13" × 9" casserole. Brush with sauce. Cover with plastic wrap, vented. MICROWAVE (high) 10–12 minutes, until meat is no longer pink and juices run clear. Let stand 3 minutes. Drain.
2. Place chicken pieces plump side down on grill, 6 inches from medium-hot coals. Brush with sauce. Do not cover grill. Grill for 3 minutes; turn pieces over and brush with sauce. Grill 3 minutes. Serve with extra sauce on the side.

SPICY MUSTARD BARBECUE SAUCE

Preparation time: 10 minutes
Microwave time: 1–2 minutes
Yield: 1 cup

¼ cup minced onion
3 tablespoons olive oil
½ cup catsup
¼ cup Dijon mustard
2 teaspoons anchovy paste

Put onion and olive oil in a 2-cup measure.
MICROWAVE (high) 1–2 minutes, until softened.
Stir in catsup, mustard, and anchovy paste.

MICRO-GRILLED SPLIT CHICKEN

Split chickens can be tricky on the grill because the pieces include both breasts and legs, which need slightly different cooking times. Cooking the pieces first in the microwave oven—in a well-lit kitchen—makes it easier to see when the chicken is done.

Preparation time: 10 minutes
Microwave time: 12 minutes
Grilling time: 10 minutes
Serves: 4

1 2- to 3-pound chicken, split through the breast

1. Start grill. Place chicken halves skin side down in a 13″ × 9″ casserole, with legs and thighs to the outside. Cover with plastic wrap, vented. MICROWAVE (high) 12–15 minutes, until meat is no longer pink and juices run clear, turning pieces over after 8 minutes. Let stand 5 minutes. Drain.
2. Place chicken pieces skin side down on grill, 6 inches from medium-hot coals. Do not cover grill. Grill for 5 minutes; turn pieces over. Grill 5 minutes.

MICRO-GRILLED WHOLE CHICKEN

In just 20 minutes, a whole chicken is cooked in the microwave oven, ready for that final wonderful finish on the grill.

Preparation time: 15 minutes
Microwave time: 21 minutes
Grilling time: 10 minutes
Serves: 6

1 3- to 3½-pound fryer
½ teaspoon salt
⅛ teaspoon freshly ground black pepper
2 tablespoons butter

1. Remove liver and neck from chicken and reserve for another use. Rinse chicken well with cold water and pat dry. Sprinkle cavity with salt and pepper.
2. Use trussing needle to sew both cavities closed. Place chicken in a 3-quart, flat casserole, breast side down. MICROWAVE (high) 10–12 minutes, to start cooking. Turn chicken over (breast side up). Cover wing tips and end of legs with smooth strips of aluminum foil to keep them from overcooking. Pour off any juices.
3. Start grill.
4. MICROWAVE (high) 10–12 minutes, until instant thermometer registers 170°F. Pour off remaining juices. Let stand, covered with foil wrap, 10 minutes, until thermometer registers 180°F.
5. Put butter in a 1-cup measure. MICROWAVE (high) 30 seconds to 1 minute to melt.
6. Place chicken, breast side down, on the grill, 6 inches above medium-hot coals. Do not cover. Baste with melted butter. Grill 5 minutes. Turn chicken over; baste. Grill 5 minutes, until skin is lightly crisp and browned.

TIP: It's OK to use foil wrap in most microwave ovens if you keep the foil smooth and at least 1 inch away from the sides of the oven.

MICRO-GRILLED WHOLE TURKEY

A small turkey is cooked in the microwave oven in less than 2 hours, then grilled a bit to crisp the skin and add some extra flavor.

Preparation time: 20 minutes
Microwave time: 1 hour, 40 minutes
Grilling time: 15 minutes
Serves: 8–10

1 10- to 12-pound turkey, fresh or defrosted
½ teaspoon salt
¼ teaspoon freshly ground black pepper
4 tablespoons (½ stick) butter

1. Remove neck and wrapped innards from turkey and reserve for another use. Rinse turkey inside and out with cold water and pat dry. Salt and pepper cavity. Use string or plastic ties to tie ends of legs together.
2. Place butter in a 1-cup measure and MICROWAVE (high) 1–2 minutes to melt. Place turkey breast side down in a 3-quart flat casserole. Brush with butter. Do not cover. MICROWAVE (medium-high) 40–45 minutes, brushing with butter and collecting pan juices twice.
3. Turn turkey over (breast side up). MICROWAVE (medium-high) 40–45 minutes, until juices run clear, basting with butter and collecting pan juices several times. Cover turkey lightly with foil wrap and let stand 15 minutes to finish cooking.
4. Start grill. Place turkey breast side down on grill 6 inches from medium-hot coals. Cover. Grill 10 minutes. Turn breast side up. Grill, uncovered, until skin is fairly crisp and brown, about 5 minutes.

TIP: *Pop-up thermometers don't always work well in a microwave oven. To test for doneness, rely on an instant meat thermometer. Take the bird out when the meatiest portion registers 170°F; during standing time it will rise to the recommended 180–185°F.*

TIP: *For more details on cooking a whole turkey, read the directions for Whole Turkey with Apple-Walnut Dressing (see Index).*

MICRO-GRILLED TURKEY BREAST WITH FRESH TOMATO SAUCE

Low-fat turkey breast is cooked first in the microwave oven, then briefly grilled and paired with a spritely fresh tomato sauce. (You can make the sauce a day ahead and store it, covered, in the refrigerator.) Note that the turkey breast is cooked in the microwave oven on medium power for even cooking. Keep the skin on during cooking to keep the meat moist; remove after grilling, if desired.

Preparation time: 10 minutes
Microwave time: 12 minutes
Grilling time: 10 minutes
Serves: 6

1 2-pound turkey breast half, boned
2 cups Fresh Tomato Sauce (recipe follows)

1. Use a veal pounder or cleaver to pound turkey breast briefly into an even thickness. Place skin side down in a 2-quart flat casserole. Cover with plastic wrap, vented. MICROWAVE (medium) 12–16 minutes, until inserted thermometer registers 170°F, turning breast over once.
2. Start grill. Let turkey breast stand on counter, lightly covered with foil, about 10 minutes, until temperature registers 180°F.
3. Place turkey breast skin side down on grill, 6 inches from medium-hot coals. Do not cover grill. Grill 5 minutes; turn turkey breast over. Grill 5 minutes. Serve with sauce on the side.

FRESH TOMATO SAUCE

Preparation time: 15 minutes
Microwave time: 15–18 minutes
Yield: 2 cups

2 pounds fresh tomatoes, peeled, seeded, and chopped coarse
1 tablespoon olive oil
½ teaspoon salt
⅛ teaspoon pepper

Put tomatoes, olive oil, salt, and pepper in a 3-quart casserole. MICROWAVE (high), uncovered, 15–18 minutes, until sauce thickens, stirring three times.

TIP: 2 pounds tomatoes = 8 small tomatoes = 3 cups chopped.

TIP: To peel a fresh tomato, use a paring knife to cut out the stem. Make an X on that same (bottom) end. Plunge the tomato into rapidly boiling water for 20–30 seconds, then rinse under cold water. Use your fingers to pull the skin off the tomato.

TIP: To seed a fresh tomato, cut the tomato in half horizontally. Hold tomato halves cut side down in palm of hands and gently squeeze out seeds over a bowl or the sink.

MICRO-GRILLED CORNISH HENS WITH NORMANDY APPLESAUCE

Little Cornish hens are speed-cooked in the microwave oven, grilled to just crisp over charcoal, and served with Calvados-spiked applesauce. A treat.

Preparation time: 10 minutes
Microwave time: 10–12 minutes
Grilling time: 10 minutes
Serves: 4

2 1- to 1¾-pound Cornish game hens
¼ teaspoon salt
⅛ teaspoon freshly ground black pepper
1 cup Normandy Applesauce (recipe follows)

1. Rinse hens well with cold water and pat dry. Salt and pepper cavities.
2. Use trussing needle to sew cavities closed. Place hens breast-side down in a 13″ × 11″ casserole, drumsticks toward the center. MICROWAVE (high) 5–6 minutes to start cooking. Turn hens over to breast side up. Cover wing tips and ends of legs with smooth strips of aluminum foil to keep them from overcooking.
3. Start grill.
4. MICROWAVE (high) 5–6 minutes, until juices run clear or instant thermometer registers 170°F. Let stand 10 minutes, or until temperature reaches 180°F.
5. Put hens breast side down on grill, 6 inches over medium-hot coals. Do not cover. Grill 5 minutes. Turn hens over. Grill 5 minutes. Cut each hen in half through the breastbone and serve skin side up, accompanied by Normandy Applesauce.

NORMANDY APPLESAUCE

Preparation time: 10 minutes
Microwave time: 8–10 minutes
Yield: 1 cup

1 pound (2–3) tart apples
   (Granny Smith or McIntosh
   are good)
2 tablespoons Calvados, or
   other brandy
2 tablespoons water
¼ teaspoon ground cinnamon
1 teaspoon sugar

Peel, core, and thinly slice apples. Put apples, Calvados, and water in a 2-quart casserole. Cover. MICROWAVE (high) 8–10 minutes, until fruit is tender, stirring once. Puree in processor if desired. Stir in cinnamon and sugar.

GRILLED DUCK WITH MANGO-RUM SAUCE

Rich-tasting duck requires only a step or two more work to cook than chicken. And the final grilling technique is the same. It's served here with a thick puree of fresh mango and rum—an exotic-tasting dish made simple in the microwave oven. (Read through the recipe for Roast Duck [see Index] for more tips on cooking duck.)

Preparation time: 10 minutes
Microwave time: 20 minutes
Grilling time: 10 minutes
Serves: 4

1 3½- to 4½-pound duck
½ teaspoon salt
¼ teaspoon freshly ground black pepper
1 cup Mango Rum Sauce (recipe follows)

1. Remove neck and giblets from duck and save for another use. Pull off and discard excess fat from cavity. Rinse duck well inside and out with cold water. Pat dry. Sprinkle salt and pepper in cavity. Use a fork to prick skin about every 2 inches. Close cavity with wooden picks. Use nylon string to tie legs together.
2. Place duck breast side down on a microwave-safe rack (a bacon rack is fine) and place rack in a large, flat casserole. Do not cover. MICROWAVE (high) 10–12 minutes to start cooking. Drain fat.
3. Start grill.
4. Turn duck over. MICROWAVE (high) 10–12 minutes, until juices run clear when thigh is pricked with a fork. Let stand 5 minutes.
5. Place duck breast side down on the grill, 6 inches above medium-hot coals. Do not cover. Grill 5 minutes. Turn duck over. Grill 5 minutes, until skin is lightly crisp and browned. Serve with Mango Rum Sauce.

TIP: Be sure to use a pan large enough to hold the fat drippings—about 2 cups from a 3- to 4-pound duck.

MANGO RUM SAUCE

Preparation time: 10 minutes
Microwave time: 10–13 minutes
Yield: 1⅓ cups

1 large, ripe mango
2 tablespoons butter
½ cup Basic Chicken Stock (see Index) or chicken broth
¼ cup rum
⅛ teaspoon ground cinnamon
2 tablespoons fresh lime juice

1. Peel and seed mango; chop the flesh into ½-inch pieces. Put chopped mango and butter in a 4-cup measure. MICROWAVE (high) 1–2 minutes to melt butter and soften fruit.
2. Stir in Basic Chicken Stock and rum. Do not cover. MICROWAVE (high) 9–11 minutes to reduce and thicken sauce, stirring twice. Stir in cinnamon and lime juice.

SAMPLE MENUS

Versatile chicken appears in many forms. Here are some suggested menus to get you started. Starred (*) dishes are recipes in this book.

Mushroom-Smothered Chicken (*)
Brown Rice
Fresh Broccoli
Frozen Strawberry Yogurt

Mom's Chicken Salad (*)
Whole-Wheat Bread
Coleslaw
Granny Smith Apples

Whole Roast Chicken with Buttermilk Gravy (*)
Mashed Potatoes
Dilled Fresh Carrots
Fresh Apricots

Spicy Chicken Gazpacho (*)
Monterey Jack Cheese
Crusty French Bread
Vanilla Custard

Sesame Chicken and Asparagus (*)
Rice
Julienned Fresh Carrots
Raspberry Sherbet

Mozzarella Chicken (*)
Spinach Noodles
Sliced Tomatoes
Spumoni

Turkey with Apple Mush (*)
Carrot Sticks
Whole-Wheat Toast
Milk
Red and Green Grapes

Chicken-Avocado Salad (*)
Bagel Chips
Lime Sherbet

Chicken-Stuffed Potatoes (*)
Tossed Salad
Fresh Apple

Ginger-Garlic Thighs (*)
Corn-on-the-Cob
Fresh Green Beans
Bread Pudding

Country-Mustard Drumsticks (*)
Potato Salad
Coleslaw
Fresh Strawberries

Almond Chicken and Rice (*)
Tossed Green Salad
Tangerines

Chicken Stroganoff (*)
Egg Noodles
Beet Salad
Baked Apples

Cabbage Dinner Soup (*)
Cheese Twist Breadsticks
Apple Pie

Raspberry-Chicken Salad (*)
Fresh Asparagus
Parker House Rolls
Frozen Lemon Yogurt

Chicken Gumbo (*)
Corn Bread
Tossed Salad
Bananas in Cream

Chicken and Mushrooms Under Blue Cheese (*)
Grilled Tomatoes
Herbed Rice
Fresh Fruit Compote

Passion Fruit Chicken (*)
Fresh Asparagus
Herbed Rice
Chocolate Eclairs

Macadamia-Chicken Salad (*)
Oatmeal Bread Toast
Lime Sherbet

Mango-Chutney Chicken Salad (*)
Chilled Herbed Rice Salad
Cheddar Cheese

Pine Nut–Stuffed Chicken Breasts (*)
Creamed Spinach
Sliced Tomato Salad
Cantaloupe

Roast Duck (*)
Turnip and Potato Puree
Brussels Sprouts
Poached Pears with Chocolate Sauce

Spicy Chicken and Shrimp Salad (*)
Sourdough Bread
Fresh Peaches

Micro-Grilled Cornish Hens with Normandy Applesauce (*)
Whole New Potatoes
Baby Peas
Fresh Raspberries

INDEX